Why Can't They Just Behave?

A Guide to Managing Student Behavior Disorders

Second Edition

Barbara F. Zimmerman, Ph.D.

Publications

LRP Publications
Horsham, Pennsylvania 19044

This publication was designed to provide accurate and authoritative information in regard to the subject matter covered. It is published with the understanding that neither the author nor the publisher is engaged in rendering legal, accounting, or other professional service. If legal advice or other expert assistance is required, the service of a competent professional should be sought.

Library of Congress Cataloging-in-Publication Data

Zimmerman, Barbara F.
  Why can't they just behave? : a guide to managing student behavior disorders / Barbara F. Zimmerman. -- 2nd ed..
      p. cm.
  Includes bibliographical references.
    ISBN 1-57834-093-4
  1. Problem children--Education--Handbooks, manuals, etc.
  2. Behavior disorders in children--Handbooks, manuals, etc. 3.
  Classroom management--Handbooks, manuals, etc. I. Title.

  LC4802.Z56   2007
  371.93--dc22

                                                      2007040324

For

My very supportive family:

Esther, my mom Janie, Ira, Judith, Mollie, Dana, Rivka and Pini

I didn't belong as a kid, and that always bothered me. If only I'd known that one day my differentness would be an asset, then my earlier life would have been much easier.

— Bette Midler

About the Author

BARBARA ZIMMERMAN, Ph.D., is a Behavior Specialist providing workshops and consultations on positive behavior management for school districts, parents, and agencies that work with children. Dr. Zimmerman has worked with behaviorally disordered and emotionally disturbed students, as well as unclassified students, from pre-school to high school levels. She also taught graduate courses in Emotional Disturbance/Behavior Disorders and Behavior Management at the College of Saint Rose in Albany, N.Y. Dr. Zimmerman holds degrees in social welfare, educational psychology/special education, and curriculum and instruction from the State University of New York at Albany.

Dr. Zimmerman's past experiences include 12 years as a classroom teacher with the Capital Region Board of Cooperative Educational Services in Albany, N.Y., working with behaviorally disordered and emotionally disturbed students from the pre-school to high school levels. Additionally, she has worked at St. Anne's Institute, a residential facility for emotionally disturbed teen-age girls, and she has taught night college courses at New York State Prisons in Wilton and Hudson, N.Y.

Dr. Zimmerman has had broad experience with disruptive behavior as a former "disrupter," a counselor, and a teacher of disruptive students. She has completed extensive research on the nature and consequences of classroom disruption and has written a chapter entitled, "Classroom Disruption: Educational Theory as Applied to

Perception and Action in Regular and Special Education," in *Advances in Special Education* (JAI Press). Dr. Zimmerman is a national speaker whose presentations and consultations include positive behavior management techniques for children who exhibit disruptive behavior, as well as general and specific ideas on positive management. Dr. Zimmerman's philosophy holds that children and adults are all individuals who have diverse needs and that optimism, a general concern for people, hard work, clear communication, and a good sense of humor are keys to obtaining positive results.

Other LRP Publications' Books by Dr. Zimmerman:

On Our Best Behavior, Second Edition (2007); *The Behavior Management Guidebook: 10 Key Training Components for Staff Development* (2003); and *The Best Fit: Creating the Right LRE for Your Students with Special Needs* (2002).

Table of Contents

Table of Contents

Table of Contents

Acknowledgments

I wish to thank the many children and adolescents I have been fortunate to work with in the past 27 years. They were, in part, the inspiration behind this book. I also wish to thank the many teachers I had as a child who supported me with kindness, firm guidance, and an ability to accommodate my unique learning and behavioral styles. I always try to forgive the teachers I had who did not possess these skills. Perhaps it is from these teachers that I developed my sense of behavior management. You can learn from everyone.

I am indebted to Jane Searle and Esther Willison who read over this text many times to ensure that my own disability did not interfere with the intent and meaning of this book. I also thank Dr. Sandra Mathison who taught me the importance of research, and I thank my editors at LRP Publications, Stephen LaRue and Maria Neithercott, who are always wonderful to work with.

This book would not have been possible without the efforts of many individuals who assisted me in my research. Their willingness to share facts, events, and experiences breathes life into this book. I am greatly appreciative of the following people: Kyle Bramer, Marge Bramer, Louise Fontaine, Jaqueline Foster, Heather Gaetano, Matthew Gaetano, Diane Hamilton, Kathy Lupi, Daphna Shamash, Sherry Shamash, Faye Tischler, Tanya Ulitsky, and Kailey Yost. I also thank the following people from the Capital Region Board of Cooperative Educational Services: Kelly Arthur, Elisa Baumeister, Judy

XV

Dyer, Stacey James, Dr. Wilma Jozwiak, Rick Lenney, Beverly Maszden, and Colleen Sullivan. Additionally, I thank Nora Rushford from The Walker Home and School in Needham, Mass., and I thank Dr. Richard Platt and Diana Rosen from Solutions: A Brief Therapy Center, located in Albany, N.Y.

I am indebted to my parents, Marvin and Natalie Zimmerman, who brought me up in a manner that greatly contributed to my exceeding any expectations I had for myself. Although my father is no longer here with me, I know he's watching out for me. I thank my brother, Ira, who always shared his toys and games with me when we were children and is a valued advisor and friend. I owe much to my sister Janie, who has always been in my corner, and who, as an adult, has made me think I can do anything. My stepdaughter and pal, Judith, is a wonderful confidant and buddy with whom I can laugh and cry.

My work environment always has been a place of enlightenment and encouragement. I am grateful to all of my colleagues at the Capital Region Board of Cooperative Educational Services. In particular, I would like to thank Ellen, Wilma, Marie, Mary, Carron, Julie, Terry and Inge. Much appreciation goes to Barbara Petraznik, who makes sure I have everything I need to do my work and much more. My association with these people furthers my enjoyment of a job that I love.

Despite my many faults, I have been fortunate to possess the ability to surround myself with wonderful friends too numerous to mention. I thank Janet, Joy, Stewart, Jackie, George, Elinor and Jill. I also thank Diana, who always knows the right thing to say for whatever mood or anxiety I am experiencing. She holds me up when I am falling down.

I thank the wonderful jewels in my life who still, gratefully, laugh at my jokes and play with me. Loving thoughts of Adam, Dana, Elise, Laura, Mollie, Pini, and Rivka. Although Spenser is no longer with us, he remains in my heart always.

Lastly, I thank Esther, my partner, who moves me in a way that no other could. She lifts me when I am disheartened and grounds me when I am flying too high.

xvii

Introduction

This book is designed for educators who work with students who have specific disabilities associated with classroom disruption. The students discussed have difficulties and problems that are not always understood, particularly since their disabilities are not physically obvious and, at times, are difficult to diagnose. This book is not meant to be an exhaustive description of causes, symptoms, and interventions of these disabilities. The intended use of this book is as a beginning reference guide for educators who, from year to year, may have some students with specific disabilities included in their program. The following disorders will be discussed:

- Attention Deficit Hyperactivity Disorder (ADHD)

- Fetal Alcohol Syndrome (FAS)

- Anxiety Disorders

- Tourette Syndrome

- Asperger Syndrome

- Traumatic Brain Injury (TBI)

- Attachment Disorder

Each chapter is divided into three sections: (1) causes and identification; (2) characteristics that affect performance and behavior in the classroom; and (3) interventions appropriate for school.

The information in this book comes from a combination of academic research and personal interviews. The research is an attempt to ascertain current theory and to provide best practices. Interviews with teachers, administrators, social workers, and other educational staff members have presented a view of these disorders and a description of specific interventions, and the interviews with students, and the parents of students with specific disabilities have allowed us a first-hand look at the struggles with which these students cope. (All names of those interviewed have been changed for purposes of confidentiality.) An additional chapter featuring parents has been added to this second edition to provide information on understanding and working cooperatively with parents of students with disabilities who have behavior disorders. Other revisions in this edition mainly reflect updated citations, research, and information on the specific disabilities and behavior management techniques discussed in this book. Citations of earlier research have been retained because I feel they still are relevant at this time.

The relationship between behavior disorders and classroom disruption is of particular interest to me due to my own personal history. I have been diagnosed with Attention Deficit Hyperactivity Disorder and, at times, when I was a child and as an adolescent, school was a difficult place for me. By the time I was in the second-grade I already had visited the school psychologist. I had the typical ADHD problems. I was impulsive, distractible, immature, too sensitive, over-active, and over-reactive. I had difficulty getting schoolwork and homework done. I felt stupid, especially in comparison to my older siblings who excelled in school. I didn't have many friends in my early school years, and I was vulnerable to teasing, which made me a prime target. I didn't feel comfortable in school and I didn't like myself very much. I felt inadequate and quite different from everyone else. I masked these feelings with an "I don't have a care in the world" attitude. By the time I was in the fourth-grade, I recognized the benefits of being a "class clown." I always looked for attention and preferred positive as opposed to negative attention. Unfortunately for me, it was easier to get the negative attention. By the time I was an adolescent I was diagnosed as hyperkinetic and later as an adult I was diagnosed with ADHD and prescribed Ritalin. I took Ritalin, as needed, and found it to be immensely helpful. Unfortunately, I had to stop taking Ritalin due to another health problem related to my lungs and heart.

Later on in my life, when I was a counselor, and then a classroom teacher, I worked with many students who had difficult behavior due to a disability or disorder. My teaching career includes one year in high school, three years in elementary and the last eight years in a middle school. Teaching suited me well. Every day was a different experience. I scheduled the day into 20- to 30-minute segments, and tried to do plenty of hands-on activities and alternated sedentary tasks with more lively activities. This type of schedule not only benefited the students, but also was perfect for me. The added bonus was that I still could be a "class clown." A good sense of humor was always an asset, whether you were a staff person or a student. My students knew that saying something humorous (as long as it didn't hurt someone's feelings, and was appropriate for school) was always rewarded. The sound of laughter can be a powerful entity.

As an adult, I still deal with the symptoms of ADHD. I'm able to cope with it better than I used to, but I have to constantly monitor myself. I still have trouble knowing where I am in space and time and therefore find it very helpful, and necessary, to surround myself with clocks, watches, and calendars. I can perseverate on ideas or events that have occurred years ago or events that will not be happening for months or even years. Changes in routine make me nervous and anxious, but I have learned to plan for them and anticipate strategies I can use. I do lots of visualization; I imagine myself in situations that are difficult for me and play them out in my head.

I am quick to overreact. I can get angry in a split-second, for example when I can't find something I'm looking for, when plans change unexpectedly, or when I'm trying to assemble something. I still have a tendency to answer a question before the person asking is finished speaking, and I have to work very hard on not interrupting people. I have difficulty being "in the moment." While I'm in the middle of one project, I'm thinking about the next project. I can now recognize when these things occur and have learned to take deep breaths, count in my head, and, when necessary and possible, to take a walk and remove myself from the situation.

I still crave variety and like new and different things. Sitting continues to be a problem so I get up often when working for long periods at a time at my desk. I seek out people with whom to chat, and I leave lots of little "mindless" tasks around to do when I take a break. I am driven

xxii

to having a project to do or to do something that I think is "useful." I live by writing lists. I've been known to write a list of my lists. I am obsessively organized, everything needs to be color-coordinated and I spend many hours reorganizing my workspace. I am a slave to this compulsion but it gives me comfort and I couldn't function without it. There are thoughts written down on pieces of paper and lists all over my house, my car and my office.

I still am impulsive. Making people laugh continues to be one of the greatest pleasures I have. I'm much better at filtering my remarks, knowing that not everything I think is funny, is funny to everyone else. Yet, as successful as I have fortunately become, I constantly fight that nagging voice in the back of my head that says, "You're stupid!"

After my own schooling experience, and 12 years of teaching, I've come to realize several things: If students do not feel safe physically and emotionally; if they do not feel respected by the person trying to teach them; and, if the curriculum is not made relevant and interesting to the students, those students will not learn. The students I worked with were difficult, yet exhilarating. There were days I came home exhausted and miserable, and there were days I came home energized and ecstatic. Some of the kids I worked with may never learn all that they "should," but they always will learn something. It seems to me that if students feel secure, comfortable, welcomed and happy, they will learn. They will learn even if you do not try to teach them anything. My classroom didn't always run smoothly, but I never expected it to. In fact, it was very often during the times when it was not running smoothly, that we all learned the most.

xxiii

Chapter One

Working with Students Who Have Behavior Disorders

Most students, in the course of their school career, occasionally will engage in inappropriate or disruptive behavior either in the classroom or somewhere in the school. I would, in fact, say that any student who goes through school and never acts out probably will experience some difficulty in adulthood, since it often is through experiencing problems and difficulties that we learn, grow, and adapt. Without early roadblocks in life an adult can become immobilized when problems arise later, having little experience and skill in dealing with such problems.

Disruption in the classroom is a well-known ingredient in school and is tolerated to a certain degree, but when the frequency and intensity of that disruptive behavior becomes great enough to impede an individual student's academic or social growth, or causes major dysfunction in the classroom, steps should then be taken to deal with that behavior and evaluate the reason for its occurrence.

Many students come to school carrying the extra baggage of having to deal with a disability or disorder that hampers or prevents them from reaching their academic or social potential. Sometimes the disorder causes behavior

1

that not only creates havoc for the individual, but also creates havoc for others in the school environment. With the current trend of integrating and including students with disabilities into general education programs, the issue of disruption in the classroom becomes even more important (Zimmerman 1995). General education teachers now have students with special needs in their classes that they did not have 10 years ago. Teachers also are subject to the pressures of the No Child Left Behind legislation. Students with special needs include, but are not limited to, students with Tourette Syndrome, Aspergers Syndrome, Attention Deficit Disorder, Traumatic Brain Injury, Anxiety Disorder, Fetal Alcohol Syndrome, and Attachment Disorder. Children and adolescents with any one of these disorders come to school with a variety of problems. These students sometimes can be mistakenly viewed by general educators, as students who simply "don't fit in." Additionally, teachers are concerned that having a student with disabilities in the class will disadvantage other students. Teachers also worry that the parents of nondisabled students will have a negative reaction to their children being in classes with students who are disabled. This is particularly true of the student with a disability who also has behavioral problems (Zimmerman 2003).

However, the benefits of inclusion have been documented. Some teachers credit inclusion with having a positive effect on everyone in a classroom. "Disabled students become more confident and independent, and their classmates learn tolerance" (Parsavand 1994, p. A1). Although it may be beneficial, inclusion, however, brings up new concerns and issues.

Teachers in inclusionary situations often feel over-whelmed by having to work with too many students with special needs. "For many of these teachers, accommodating the students' academic and behavioral difficulties requires considerable effort or may even necessitate instructional expertise they have not yet acquired" (Heckman and Rike 1994, p. 30). The American Federation of Teachers has publicly stated their opposition to full inclusion, pointing out that teachers are not adequately trained to deal with the wide range of disabilities, physical and emotional (Feldman 1994).

Clare Royal was a special education teacher for 17 years and served as a special education coordinator for three years. She also was an elementary school principal. Currently she is the director of Special Education for a midsize urban district. She discussed the benefits of including students with disabilities into regular education programs —

> *When you include students with special needs into general education programs the children as well as the professionals are exposed to the fact that students do not come in "one-size-fits-all." Students begin to accept others who are different. They also begin to see that, although these students may have labels, or special equipment or different ways in which they behave, they are more like themselves than different. I think it's a win-win situation for both groups of kids. They learn from each*

3

*other. They realize that there are a lot of
people who make up this world.*

Having students with disabilities in the classroom can
add an extra burden to the general education teacher,
Royal acknowledged —

> *I think the difficulty is that in this day and
> age when we are trying to "raise the bar,"
> to raise standards, and try to do more with
> less (teachers have larger class sizes, the
> curriculum is more intense), time seems to
> be a problem for teachers. They want to do
> the right thing for all kids, but they feel
> there is not enough time to collaborate and
> to do the job fully. In many ways teachers
> feel overwhelmed.*

Teachers need to be supported when they have students who have disabilities in their classrooms, particularly those students who have behavioral problems. Royal
elaborated —

> *Schools need to do their homework. By this
> I mean, the building administrator, the
> social worker, the psychologist, and the
> ancillary staff really need to have some
> prerequisite knowledge of the child with
> special needs. We can do some groundwork
> with and for the teacher. We can start the
> wheels turning to develop a good behavior
> plan. We can provide training for the
> teacher. My role is to be a sounding board*

for the teachers. I need to be a good listener. We need to reach out of our four walls and hook up with other professionals. I share research articles and tips from other teachers. I share ideas from my own classroom experience. I give teachers release time to look at other classes and other programs, and I sometimes go in and model teaching methods.

It should be noted, however, that in any event, issues of disruption, whether caused by the classroom environment or caused by individual students, need to be addressed. The time has come to start training all teachers, special and regular educators, in the same manner (Zimmerman 2007). All teachers should be trained to work with students with and without disabilities.

The behavior of one individual usually is judged by other individuals. There is clearly no "normal" way to behave. Behavior is contextual, and depending on where the behavior takes place, who is witnessing it, and what the cause of it is, the behavior will be deemed acceptable by some and unacceptable by others. Example: Screaming on the playground is acceptable; screaming in the classroom is not.

When there are chronic behavior problems associated with a student, an evaluation of some sort usually takes place, and a label often is assigned. Labels are a good example of a "necessary evil." Without a label, students are unable to get necessary services, or are frustrated by expectations that they cannot meet — emotionally or cognitively. Labels, however, can be stigmatizing and some-

5

times impede a student's ability to reach his or her potential. Royal stated that many of the problems that arise in inclusion situations begin with the stigma attached to having a disability. She further stated that people have preconceived notions and the fear of the unknown. This can cloud a teacher's judgment and ability.

Sometimes students are labeled because their behavior does not meet the standards specific to their culture or the social institutions in their environment, such as in their school. Great care should be taken when labeling any student. "While there is inevitably a negative and hostile aspect to the naming and valuing of behavior as 'disturbing, disturbed, or disordered,' there is frequently also something positive and well-intentioned. It is this duality of valence in our definition of others as in need of special services that sparks the continuing debate about its morality. It is when the positive aspect is weak or missing that defining slips into mere labeling. We cannot fully understand the ethical dilemma we face as special educators unless we recognize the mingling, in any act of definition of both positive and negative elements" (Wood 1979, p. 4).

The first step in dealing with students with disabilities is acquiring a full understanding of an individual student's specific disability. This understanding will facilitate the teacher's ability to design and implement a successful and meaningful program for that student. Educators usually are among the first people to notice what they consider to be behavior that does not fall within the "normal range." "Faced with the discrepancy between how people behave and how we expect them to behave, we derive our own hypotheses" (Streissguth 1999, p. 106).

Disabilities vary and the characteristics of each are different, therefore the interventions may be different. It should be noted, however, that even among students who have the same disability there can be differences in characteristics and in how these students act and respond to interventions. Diagnosis is key in determining what is going on with any student. Since educators are not trained in medical diagnosis, and it is inappropriate for an educator to make such a diagnosis, the disabilities discussed in this book must be determined by a physician. If an educator suspects that there is a problem with a student, it is important for that person to recommend an evaluation to determine if the student is suffering from a disability. The evaluation could yield important information as to what interventions would be appropriate for that student. Once a full understanding of the disability has been gained, the educator must then understand the unique needs of each individual student. As previously mentioned, all students with a specific disability will not have the same symptoms, reactions or characteristics. Programming and intervention should be based on the specific difficulty the student may be encountering.

When a teacher notices a child because that child "stands out," how that teacher approaches the parent of that child is crucial. Again, teachers should never "diagnose" a child with a specific disability and they certainly should never recommend to a parent that a child take medication. This is clearly a medical decision. If the teacher suspects that a student has a certain disability, such as

7

Attention Deficit Hyperactivity Disorder or Aspergers Syndrome, he or she should go through the usual channels and procedures followed by the school district. This usually involves a child study team or an evaluation by some other appropriate personnel. After an evaluation, a student often is recommended to the Committee on Special Education where he or she is then classified with a specific disability. With this classification, appropriate modifications should be designed and employed by the educational staff members who work with the student to assist that student in the most beneficial way.

When speaking to the parent it is best for the teacher not to make sweeping statements such as, "He appears to be hyperactive." It is best to simply describe the behavior very specifically such as, "John is unable to sit in his seat for more than five minutes at a time, and he has difficulty remaining quiet during lesson periods." If there are specific difficulties, the child will benefit from a united approach to dealing with the problems. If the parents feel that the teacher has the best interest of their child at heart, they are much more likely to work with the teacher in a cooperative spirit. This requires patience and understanding from both the educators and the parents. "Maintaining a supportive attitude rather than one that is accusatory or defensive will encourage parents to participate in the partnership. Facilitating the parent-school relationship is important as this alliance will allow schools to better serve the needs of the student" (Streissguth 1999, p. 214).

According to Royal, educators need to understand not only what the child is going through, but also what the family, as a whole, is experiencing —

*I really emphasize with teachers that they
need to empathize with all children. You
have to look at some situations from the
family's and child's points of view. What do
they struggle with? What are they dealing
with?*

When a child is medically diagnosed with a specific disability, the family of that child may go through a myriad of emotions. Sometimes parents are in denial about problems, or feel a sense of loss. However, they may feel relief after a diagnosis finally is determined. The parents may learn that the behavioral difficulties their child is experiencing do not necessarily mean that they are poor parents. (It should be noted that children with disabilities who come from families that are dysfunctional will experience a greater amount of stress related to their disability.) The children may feel a sense of relief knowing the problem is not that they are "bad" or that they are "troublemakers," and in the best of circumstances, those children gain empathy and understanding from those with whom they work. Educators can assist parents by helping them locate resources for dealing with the specific disabilities of their child.

Parents can become hostile toward, or overly demanding of, the educator. This is understandable since every parent wants the best for his or her child. Additionally, parents sometimes are left out of "the loop" and feel that they are not given an opportunity to participate in the educational programming of their child. Educators can help relieve parents' fears by assuring them that they will do everything possible for their children. Enlisting parents to help solve problems is a good way to start a beneficial working process. Ask parents what they have tried with their children in the past, or what they have found works for them. Involve them in using the specific management strategies that you, as the educator, have found useful. Develop a spirit of cooperation and mutual respect. Parents are a valuable source, according to Royal —

> *We need to form a strong partnership with parents because parents are their kids' first teacher. Many of the parents know "tricks of the trade" when it comes to their own children.*

(More information on working with and assisting parents of students with disabilities and behavior problems will be discussed in Chapter Three.)

When a student is diagnosed and classified with a disability, common sense should prevail. Developing the appropriate modifications is not an easy task. If we under-modify for the student, there is a risk of creating undo frustration for that student. Under-modification involves having expectations that the student is either emotionally or cognitively unable to meet (e.g., sitting too long with a paper and pencil task, assigning material that is at grade-level, but too difficult for the student). If we over-modify, we give those students the message that they are not as competent as they are. Furthermore, you run the risk of those students developing a dependence on a "crutch" they do not need. Over-modification could include not allowing a student, who is socially able, to eat in the cafeteria with peers or having someone take notes for students who are capable of taking their own notes. Some programs may not be successful because of poor implementation. This should be assessed first. Inconsistency in implementation of the program, no matter how well designed the program is, often results in a program's failure (Divack, Herrie and Scott 1985). Sometimes, as educators, we are too quick to change a program when a simple fine-tuning would eradicate difficulties that are being experienced. It is well-documented that consistency is essential in working with any student who has behavioral difficulties (Zimmerman 1998, 2007). Changing implementation plans often will confuse and upset a student, creating more behavioral difficulties.

Working with children is a challenging experience, particularly, working with children who have the additional burden of having a disability. It is important to remember that progress can be a slow and painful journey for the teacher, but more importantly, for the child. "Impatience is perhaps the greatest enemy which must be dealt with. In the desire to see results, and in too many cases, immediate results, we manage to do the child in need the greatest harm. We need time to work toward the solutions that will be of most benefit to the children with whom we must deal. It takes time to establish relationships, time to create an environment of support and trust, time to heal old wounds, time to reshape thinking, time to note even imperceptible change, time to continue in the belief that change and improvement are possible" (Teitelbaum 1979, p. 91). General educators, who may have as many as 20 or 30 students in their classroom, find that the task of teaching a child with a disability can seem staggering. "Teach-

11

ers may develop unrealistic expectations, frustration, and anger as well as feelings of helplessness and guilt" (Tucker and Colson 1992, p. 206).

To be able to work effectively with a student who has disabilities it is critical that we understand what that student goes through on a daily basis. Educators, need to be able to "get into the sneakers" of these students. A 23-year-old graduate student, in a course assignment, wrote about her childhood experiences as a disabled child in school —

> *Everyone wants to be understood. Our society establishes a norm. Those who don't fit into this mold feel alone, frustrated, and confused. These feelings often result from other people not understanding what they are going through. Normal to me was to be so terrified to read in class that I could not pronounce words like "said" and "the." Normal to me was beginning to read a passage in class and having my hands shake so badly that I could not keep my place on the page. Normal to me was reading out loud and hearing the other students laughing and making comments. Normal to me was walking into a test with extreme anxiety and then going completely blank when the paper was put in front of my face. Normal to me was to read a multiple-choice question five times because someone dropped his pencil or coughed. Normal to me was taking four hours to read*

*one chapter without being able to under-
stand the concepts. Normal to me was having teachers thinking I didn't study enough.
Normal to me was screaming inside, frustrated because I was unable to come up
with the right words to say that would
make someone understand.*

The goal is to enable the student with a disability "to function with the greatest degree of independence possible, with the best quality of life, and in the least restrictive environment" (Deaton 1994, p. 258). When educating any child it is important to step back and look at the "big picture." What are our hopes for the child being educated? Teaching children the ability to think for themselves so that they can be as independent as possible should be high on the list. Ultimately, however, to love and be loved is the most important component of being human. The question remains — How do we help students, particularly students who have disabilities and behavioral disorders, achieve this essential element in life?

Although the task of working with students with disabilities is difficult, so many times these children enhance the classroom in ways that the educator never imagined they could.

13

Chapter Two

Classroom Management

It is important to recognize that even if a child has a disability we do that child a dreadful disservice if we excuse any inappropriate behavior. Perhaps the greatest skill we can teach all children is the skill of taking responsibility for one's own behavior. If individuals do not take responsibility for their behavior, someone else will.

Certainly, there will be times when children will not be able to control their actions. However, children also learn how to manipulate and make excuses for behavior that they can control. Granted, it can be difficult to distinguish between intentional and unintentional behavior.

Behaviors that a student cannot control require instruction or development of a strategy for compensation. Noncompliant behavior requires disciplinary techniques designed to teach compliance. The goal, then, is not to create individuals who will blindly do all that they are told to do, but to teach students to learn and understand that at times in their life they will have to do things that they either don't agree with, find hard to do, or just do not want to do (McNamara 1996). This is a fact of life that applies to everyone in our society. A student who never learns to be compliant when it is necessary will have a difficult life. It is essential to teach students to co-exist with their disability and to compensate for their weaknesses.

15

Perhaps the most important thing we can teach students is how to gain insight into themselves. Personal insight provides valuable information for students so that they can learn what it is that makes them upset, at what times or when they get upset, and what works best for them when they are getting upset or already have reached that point.

Many of the interventions and environmental alterations that will be discussed in this book would benefit most students, regardless of whether they have a disability or not. The crucial thing to remember is that many students with a disability or disorder cannot survive without the necessary interventions or environmental alterations.

The best method of preventing disruption in the classroom is to provide activities and lessons that are engaging and relevant to the student. When a student is actively engaged in an interesting activity he or she is less apt to engage in disruptive behavior.

Unfortunately, there are many roadblocks to creating interesting and relevant curriculum and instruction. Although, unintentional, the No Child Left Behind Act of 2002 has caused some serious instructional problems, particularly for students who have disabilities. "The No Child Left Behind act in theory, is one of the greatest educational creations, but not in implementation. The single most appalling problem with this is act is its lack of funding. Essentially, we are creating great test-takers and poor learners" (Lentini 2007).

Since many students who have disabilities also have learning deficits, it is important to teach at the academic level of the individual student. If this is not done, a student usually will not participate in the lesson. All students should be instructed in a range of 95 percent to 97 percent known material and no more than 3 percent to 5 percent new or unknown material. This means building on existing skills. When students are instructed at their independent levels (more than 97 percent known material, which should be used for only independent practice), they become bored and may be disruptive. When they are instructed at their frustration levels (94 percent of lesser known material), they become frustrated, tune out, and may become disruptive.

In order to make education relevant, it is necessary to teach students in relation to the experiences that he or she brings to school from home and community.

"Often the material is not translated into life-terms, but is directly offered as a substitute for, or an external annex to, the child's present life. The following three typical evils result: 1. Lack of organic connection with what the child has already seen, felt and loved makes the material purely formal and symbolic. Without preliminary activities the symbol is bare, dead, barren. 2. Lack of motivation. 3. Even the most scientific matter, arranged in most logical fashion loses this quality when presented in external, ready-made fashion. It becomes 'stuff for memory'" (Dewey 1902, pp. 24-26).

Dewey felt that schools were not adequately utilizing the students' abilities and community experiences and that the education provided to students was not useful in terms of the students' lives. "The great waste in the school comes from the student's inability to utilize the experiences he gets outside of school in any complete and free way within the school itself; while on the other hand he is

17

unable to apply in daily life what he is learning in school. Natural connections should be made between the child's experience and education" (Dewey 1900, p. 75). Dewey felt that students should be guided, but that education should be self-directed. In terms of handling disruptive behavior, perhaps Dewey would have felt the same, that students should be guided but the handling of disruptive behavior should be self-directed. All that the student needs is an interest. "Impulse or interest means to work it out, and working it out involves running up against obstacles, becoming acquainted with materials, exercising ingenuity, patience, persistence, alertness, it, of necessity, involves discipline — ordering of power — and supplies knowledge. (All the more better that the child is motivated. By necessity he will learn the discipline, since [it is needed] to solve the problem.) For the child to realize his own impulse by recognizing the facts, materials and conditions involved, and then to regulate his impulse through that recognition is education" (Dewey 1902, pp. 39-41).

Before designing and implementing any behavior plan for any individual student the educator needs to understand, and be empathetic to, the needs of that student. "It often helps to remember that children with difficult behavior do not stay up all night thinking of ways to torture the adults in their lives, even though at times this is exactly what these adults think. Disruptive children want what most children want: to be accepted, loved and validated. Something in the disruptive child's life short-circuits this goal" (Zimmerman 2007, p. 13). "No matter how bad a child's behavior seems, it is important to remember that most children are driven to succeed and that at any given time they are probably doing the best they can with the abilities they have" (Deaton 1994, p. 258).

Understanding the function, or purpose of any inappropriate behavior is the necessary first step in dealing with that behavior. "By recognizing the message behind the behavior, the educator can respond more effectively to these needs and also help the student learn appropriate methods of communicating his or her needs. Students who inappropriately express their needs are often misunderstood and ridiculed, or goaded by fellow students and viewed as troublemakers by administrators and teachers. Teaching these students to shape their inappropriate behaviors into appropriate words and actions is perhaps even more useful to the student's success in life than a specific math concept or lesson in grammar" (Streissguth 1999, p. 219). Another important aspect of analyzing the function of the behavior is to ascertain where and when this behavior is occurring and where and when it is not occurring. "Systematic observation of the student's social/emotional status in a variety of settings is a logical first step in planning appropriate intervention strategies" (Tucker and Colson 1992, p. 205).

It is vital that we teach children with disabilities, who cause disruptive behavior, the social skills that are essential in making their way in the world. These students need to recognize when they are having difficulty and when they need or want something. They also should learn how to ask for what they need and want in an appropriate manner, and how to deal with getting it or not getting it. Most importantly, students with disabilities should learn to live with the baggage they carry. It often is difficult for educa-

19

tors to teach social and behavioral skills that they did not need to learn. Breaking down these skills for a student with social and/or behavioral problems can be a daunting task, but one that is essential. The teaching always has to begin where the student is ready to learn. The educator must be aware of the student's limitations and the student's strengths. There will be more success when instruction utilizes the strengths of that student, which, in turn, will increase the student's level of motivation and achievement.

Working with students with difficult behavior can be annoying and infuriating. "Very often, when a child is presenting difficult behavior, this begins to dominate our thinking, and we can lose sight of his strengths, abilities and progress in other areas. A spiral of anxiety, anger and concern may develop and lead to a distorted perception of the problem. This will only make intervention more difficult" (Cumine, Leach and Stevenson 1998, p. 66).

Different types of interventions for students with disabilities will be discussed in this book. Each student is an individual and requires individual interventions. (Specific interventions are discussed in Chapter Eleven.) There are, however, some basics in behavior management that are useful for all students.

Structure and consistency are important for all students, but crucial for students with chronic behavior difficulties. These students must learn limitations and experience the consequences when their actions go beyond those limitations. On some level it is a tightrope act. As an educator, you may find yourself asking, "Am I being too rigid or am I being too lenient?" You'll get clues to the answers for these questions by the response you get from the student. It can be vexing because the student tends to resist structure, or what he may see as constraints; yet, without this structure students can become lost, frustrated and even hostile.

Consistency is critical and as important as structure in working with students with behavior problems because they are not able to predict their environment as successfully as other students, and they will rely on consistency and set patterns established in the classroom. Additionally, they are not good observers of others' behavior (or their own), nor do they have a good sense of time. As a result, they cannot anticipate events, unless a consistent and well-publicized plan is in place. Changes in routine and changes in the way behavior is handled usually send a student with behavior problems into a tailspin.

Once the structure and consistency are built into the program, follow-through is crucial. The student must see consequences for both appropriate and inappropriate behavior. "These consequences should be delivered in a calm and swift manner" (Zimmerman 2007).

Follow-through is essential to maintaining structure and consistency. It is one of the major factors that contribute to a calm environment. The teacher must follow through on consequences for not only the big infraction, but the little ones as well. (Zimmerman 2007). McEwan and Damer (2000) state, "Tackling the small stuff while it is still manageable will foster a school environment in which the catastrophic problems are far less likely to occur." (p. 8). It has always been my opinion that it is better to have no rule than to have a rule that is not enforced.

21

The student with behavior problems must see consequences for both appropriate and inappropriate behavior, and these consequences should be delivered in a calm and swift manner.

Structure and flexibility are two vital components of discipline. "Structure, a very important component of effective discipline, refers to a clear and consistent emphasis on predictability. Difficult children invariably do better if they know what is expected of them, provided the expectations don't change constantly" (Turecki 2000, p. 131). While it is important to be very structured and to set limits with follow-through, there must be a degree of flexibility involved as well. As with most things, using common sense is always a good idea.

Chapter Three

Working Together
and Assisting Parents

Educators can play a vital role in assisting parents of students with disabilities in creating a positive home environment. A positive home environment will help the student not only at home, but will help that student adapt better to the demands of school. Additionally, when educators and parents work together in a spirit of cooperation both the educators and the parents gain valuable information and strategies.

Many of the strategies used in the classroom can be modified and can be useful at home. Teachers have many responsibilities so it can be difficult for them to find the time to do everything.

Working with parents can be extremely time-consuming; however, when a good relationship is forged between school and home the results usually are beneficial for the educators, the parents, and most importantly, the student.

It is extremely important for educators who are working with parents of children with disabilities to understand these parents. The reactions and responses of parents with disabled children are, of course, quite varied. Some parents are in denial about their child's disability, or the severity of the disability. Some parents believe their child

23

is more disabled than he really is. Some parents withhold information from the educators, while other parents inundate educators with material about their child and about their child's disability. Educators must be sensitive to the added pressures that come with having a disabled child. "Parents often have to spend time and energy taking their child to doctors or counselors, attending meetings at school, or supervising their child at home and in the community" (Marsh 2007, p. 170).

It is essential for all educators working with a student with a disability to educate themselves thoroughly about the disability. It can be quite upsetting for a parent when they realize the professionals do not have all the information they need to appropriately educate their child.

"Connecting with a family is important with any child, but it's especially important where challenging behavior is concerned. It's simply too hard to understand and manage behavior problems in a vacuum. Families know their child best, and their insight and collaboration can be invaluable. They can tell you about their lives and their culture — family roles, origin, support network, patterns of authority — and about such stress factors as illness divorce, and money problems" (Kaiser and Sklar Raminsky 2003, p. 213).

Parent conferences are extremely important. Keeping communication lines open and positive can be essential for the development and implementation of a student's academic and behavioral program. Starting a parent conference in a positive manner yields greater cooperation from parents. "One of the first messages you should communicate during a parent conference is that you care about their child. When parents realize you appreciate and value their son or daughter, they are more likely to work cooperatively with the school. Remember, parents see their child as a reflection of themselves. Consequently, when you compliment a student, you are also complimenting the parents" (Boynton and Boynton 2005, p. 93).

Equally important is encouraging parents to communicate with the school when they have questions, comments, or concerns. "Far too often, parents hear rumors about school incidents that make no sense. Most of the time, this information is inaccurate. When parents do not contact the school to check the stories out, they can form negative opinions about the school or a teacher. In an effort to head off these situations, teachers and administrators should continually urge parents to contact the school any time they have questions or concerns that bother them. When doing so, let the parents know that the school welcomes and appreciates these questions" (Boynton and Boynton 2005, p. 95). To facilitate this type of communication parents should be provided with building and classroom phone numbers and the best times to call. Parents should be informed that staff members may not be able to return calls immediately due to the busy schedule of teaching. However, teachers and administrators should return the calls in as timely a manner as possible.

It is, at times, difficult for the educator to talk with parents about the inappropriate behavior of their children. Discussions need to be sensitively addressed so that the parent does not feel threatened and does not become defensive. As a teacher, it was my policy to make the first discussion with a parent a positive one. (For some of my students that meant calling their parents on the first day of school.) It is important to be clear, direct, and non-judgmental. It is best to talk about a specific behavior, such as a student's difficulty in completing assignments. Avoid making sweeping statements such as, "Johnny is lazy." This may put off a parent. It is always important for teachers to remember that the better the relationship with a student's parent, the better that student will do in school.

There will be times when educators will need to deal with unhappy and/or angry parents. Dealing with angry parents takes patience and self-control. It also requires practice. Boynton and Boynton (2005) suggest the following when meeting with angry parents:

1. Let the parent vent.

2. Remain calm, don't get defensive.

3. Maintain eye contact

4. Communicate you are listening (e.g., take notes).

5. Let the parent get to his or her agenda first.

6. Discuss the future (i.e., don't get hung up on the past).

7. End abusive conferences gracefully and swiftly.

8. Admit mistakes.

Parents need to be included in the process of educating their disabled child and in the process of dealing with inappropriate behavior. "When parents and educators come to the table to discuss problem behaviors, it is important to adopt a team approach. The decisions of the team must come from a systematic approach to looking at the behavior. Once methods are put in place to address this behavior, they must be adopted and used by everyone who works with the student. Just as parents must be in agreement with the way they handle behavior problems at home, parents and teachers must be in agreement with the way they are handled at school. If the student's plan is to be effective for him/her, it must be adopted and supported by everyone who works with him/her" (Moyes 2004, p. 19).

Kaiser and Sklar Raminsky (2003) documented a school-based study that shows that parents are more likely to become involved in a child's education if they believe that they can help their child succeed. They also are more likely to get involved if they believe that the teacher's invitation is serious and sincere and that their child wants them there.

27

Parents Appreciate Teachers When:

- The teacher respects their opinions and implements their ideas.

- The teacher treats them as equal participants in their child's education.

- The teacher responds promptly to calls.

- The teacher keeps promises and explains delays.

- The teacher says positive things about their child.

Parents Become Upset and Lose Trust in Teachers When:

- The teacher fails to communicate with them.

- The teacher becomes defensive (e.g., the teacher gets upset when a parent questions a grade or asks to see his child's records).

- The teacher stonewalls them. (Making a promise to do something and not following through.)

- The teacher over-reacts.

- The teacher uses stereotypes based on marital status, socio-economic status, etc.

- The teacher is unwilling to try a different approach.

- The teacher is unwilling to apologize and admit mistakes.

Even in the best of all possible relationships between school and home there is the possibility that problems can arise. Something important to keep in mind is that just as it is unreasonable for parents to expect the teacher to be able to do everything they may ask him to do, it is just as unreasonable for the teacher to expect the parents to be able to do everything they are asked to do.

It is important to be proactive in dealing with parents about discipline problems that may arise. "When you discipline or correct a student, there is always the possibility the student will give his or her parents a skewed version of what happened. Students typically leave out critical information in an effort to make it appear that they did nothing wrong and were treated unfairly. Often parents buy students' stories and become upset with you. On some situations, the issue festers until a parent angrily contacts the school to deal with you. At this point, you are faced with the difficult task of calming the parents down and presenting the correct facts" (Boynton and Boynton 2005, p. 93.).

As mentioned previously, having a child with behavior problems due to a disability causes a family tremendous stress. "In their (parents') minds, having a child with behavior problems is a sign they aren't good parents, and they feel embarrassed, isolated, rejected, and stigmatized by other parents whose children seem perfect. Their own extended family often criticizes the way they discipline the child, making numerous unsupportive suggestions that evoke even more unease and guilt" (Kaiser and Sklar Raminsky 2003, pp. 214-215). Under these circumstances educators can suggest some assistance for families to ease this stress.

29

Support groups with other families who have children with the same disability as their own child can be wonderful for parents. They provide a forum to vent frustrations that are easily understood by others. Support groups also can be a great place for families to pick up successful strategies that other families use. Additionally, and maybe most importantly, parents who are involved in support groups find out that they are not alone and feel much less alienated.

Another valuable resource for families is counseling to assist the family with the unique needs of the disabled individual. Counseling also can provide the strategies and coping mechanisms to deal with that individual. When suggesting counseling try not to present the idea in a judgmental manner. When counseling is suggested by educators, parents sometimes get defensive thinking that the teacher thinks they are bad parents. Even if the parents are not terribly skilled, an educator should not put the parents on the defensive.

Providing Strategies to Parents

It will be helpful for the teacher to keep in mind that being a parent is not an easy job. Many parents feel the task of raising children is like walking the high wire without a net. There are so many decisions to make — small and large. Parents often find themselves wondering if they are being too strict or too lenient, and they may ask themselves such questions as the ever popular, "If Susie's mother is letting her go, should I let my kid go too?" Sometimes there is more than one acceptable answer, and sometimes there is no answer at all. The fact of the matter is that being a parent is hard work. It is an emotional, physical, and sometimes even a spiritual journey that requires careful planning, support and, most importantly, a sense of humor.

Raising a child can be an extremely challenging yet rewarding experience. Dealing with a child with behavior difficulties can be more challenging, requiring a great deal of thoughtful planning on the part of the parent. Educators can remind parents of two key elements — try to keep your cool and try to keep a sense of humor. Children count on their parents to be in control. Although that may not always be possible, the parent needs to learn what to do to stay calm. Sometimes it may be necessary to take a break, a walk, a run, a bike ride, or any other activity. Activities are great ways to blow off steam appropriately.

Every parent at one time or another feels that she is not in control of the situation. Often parents are frustrated because they simply don't know what to do. It's at these times that the high wire begins to shake. Knowing that there is a reliable and considerate educator who can assist is beneficial for the parent — it's the safety net under that high wire.

At home, as in the classroom, there are two ingredients that need to balance with each other — consistency and nurturance. To explain what that means requires some deeper understanding of each concept. Again, the educator can provide support for parents in these key areas.

Consistency

Consistency and structure encompass several components — setting limits, rules and follow-through. It is

31

much easier to provide this type of environment in a classroom than in a home, but not impossible. Not only will children feel more comfortable in this environment, parents also will. Consistency eliminates the need for parents to "reinvent the wheel" every time there is a problem.

Most children, and adults too, respond best in a predictable environment. When individuals feel that they are not in control, then they try to control everything. Parents often notice their child's behavior becomes difficult when the routine is disrupted. That is why family vacations can be so harrowing or why when visitors stay over children become cranky. Routine is developed through the structure of daily living, which is why it is not always possible to provide as much consistency as is necessary. I have heard many people say, "life often gets in the way of our plans." Things happen that we cannot always predict.

Setting Limits

It's a comfort to a child to know someone responsible is in charge who will not let things get out of control. (However, do not expect any child to admit this!) The child must be clear on "how far" he can go. If there are no limits, he will not have any idea when to stop, and this can lead to some significant disruptive behavior. Setting limits can be a difficult task because we don't always know what the limits should be. It requires some introspection.

First, parents need to know their own limits. For example, consider the parents' tolerance level for dealing with a whining child. Is their tolerance level limited to 5 minutes of whining or 20 minutes, or no whining at all? Once parents know the answer to that question they must figure out realistic and acceptable expectations for their child. Is it reasonable to expect your child to whine for 5 minutes or 20 minutes, or does the situation call for no whining at all? The parent also must take into account the situation in which the behavior is occurring. Tolerance levels will change depending on where the parent is, what time of day it is, and other factors that affect behavior.

Rules

Rules should be clear and direct. The child should understand what he is supposed to do and why he is expected to do it. Rules should be reasonable and achievable. Parents sometimes set up their child for failure by asking him to do things of which he may not be capable of doing (e.g., expecting a 5-year-old child to sit in Uncle Harry's living room for more than a half-hour watching vacation slides of Egypt). The child should have a voice in making the rules. Just like adults, children will be more prone to adhere to rules they helped create. It is important that everyone, adult and child, feels they have some control. For one person to have all the power is never a good idea. Others start to feel resentful and may become oppositional. If a parent has all the power the child learns not to approach the parent to get his needs met because he feels that it's a waste of time and a useless venture. But giving the child all the power can be dangerous for a number of reasons. Children do not always use the best judgment; they also need to learn to seek adult advice; and, a child who expects and demands everything to go his own way all of the time is impossible to live with. The parent could become a hostage as the child resorts to physical and emo-

33

tional blackmail to get what he wants. ("If you don't get me this toy I'm going to scream and yell as loud as I can in this very public place.") Additionally, this does not prepare a child to become a cooperative member of society. I have often found that a child who has always gotten his way starts to resent the parent. On some level, he feels that the parent didn't care enough about him to set limits, such as setting a bedtime. By the time the child is 8 years old, he may start to give the parent a hard time by being oppositional.

In reality no one gets their own way all of the time. Children need to learn how to state their needs, negotiate for what they want, compromise when necessary, and deal with the outcome of the situation. If a child learns and uses these skills he will have a greater chance of living a successful life.

Follow-through

Follow-through on consequences is often difficult for parents. It is important for educators to help parents understand that, if rules are broken, there must be a consequence or these rules will be broken again. This also is true for rewarding appropriate behavior. If an agreement is made between a child and a parent for a reward for certain behavior, the reward must be given if the child lives up to his end of the bargain. When follow-through is nonexistent, or inconsistent, children learn not to trust the parent or, worse, not to take the parent seriously. Once children lose trust in a parental figure it becomes difficult for them to trust other adults in their lives. This could include educators who make academic and behavioral demands on the children.

At times it is difficult to follow-through. Parents may feel that their children will hate them if they deliver a consequence, and children may reinforce this feeling by actually saying, "I hate you," in hopes of getting what they want. Sometimes parents may feel that it's not worth the effort or energy to follow-through with specified consequences for inappropriate behavior. The problem is that children will learn they can get away with things that they are not supposed to do, and this will become the norm for the child. If the rule, for instance, is that the child has a 9 o'clock bedtime on school nights, then that is the time the child should go to bed (unless there is an extraordinary circumstance, the parent should stick to this time). If the parent allows the child to dawdle, or if there is always a reason why the child cannot get into bed by 9:00 p.m., he will learn that there really is no set bedtime and the bedtime then becomes however late the child can push it before the parent loses patience.

Becoming lax on follow-through can have several negative effects on parents. Parents eventually get tired of fighting with their children and sometimes give up entirely. This can create a disruptive and sometimes dangerous environment for children who, without the proper guidance and supervision, may act out of control. A parent also may build up resentment and hostility toward his child causing the parent to lose control. Children can be cooperative, but it is the parent who has to take the lead. If a parent is fair and follows through this will be exactly what the child learns.

Consequences, as mentioned previously, are extremely important. However, you do not want to humiliate or make your child feel worthless. Parents should avoid name calling or using expressions such as "bad boy" or "bad girl." Parents need to understand that the idea behind a consequence is to express dislike of a behavior, not dislike of their child (Turecki 2000).

When parents follow through appropriately, their job as a parent becomes easier. When parents "stick to their guns" the child will eventually learn not to argue knowing that the parent means business and no amount of pleading, begging, whining, or yelling will change the decision.

Nurturance

When parents nurture their children they are showing them love, care, and attention. It is this unconditional love that tells the child, "I may not always like your actions or behavior, but I will always love you, no matter what." A nurturing home provides a safe haven for the child where he can be who he is without fear of harm or humiliation.

Essentially, nurturing is the parents' way of taking care of their child, supplying the things that the child needs to grow — love, food, shelter, and encouragement. A key element for parents in this process is accepting and validating their child's feelings by giving him opportunities to state his hopes, dreams, and fears.

As with everything, a balancing act usually is required for a parent to be successful in nurturing his child. Every child is different and will require different things. As an example, think about a child's first visit to the ocean. Some children will be afraid to go into the water so the situation would require the parent to find a way to reassure and "ease" the child into the water. The parent could venture into the water first, then he could carry the child in, and eventually, the child could walk in while holding the parent's hand and, finally, the child would walk in independently. However, some children, upon seeing the water for the first time, may run in recklessly unaware of the potential danger. The nurturing parent must take a different tack with this child, by slowing him down and demonstrating how to enjoy the water while respecting the potential danger.

If parents find that it is sometimes difficult to nurture their child the educator should reassure them by letting the parents know that they are not alone in having these feelings. Children take a great deal of time and energy. They often are self-absorbed and demanding, and don't always recognize their parents' emotional or physical limitations. Children can be all-consuming. When a parent has been up night after night with a child who is suffering with an earache, it is normal to want to escape the house, run away, and join the circus.

Parents cannot be all things to their child at all times. It may be necessary to take a break or seek help and support from others. This does not mean that the parent is inept. It simply means that the parent is human. Turning to trusted educators, friends, or siblings who have children of the same age can help since most other parents have gone through similar experiences.

The Consistency/Nurturance Combination

Now that the essential ingredients to good parenting have been discussed, here is the dilemma. Consistency and nurturance usually do not go hand in hand. People who are highly consistent and structured without being nurturing also may be rigid, distant, or even unrelenting. This causes children to become resentful of these adults or even afraid of them. And then again, people who are nurturing but are unable to be consistent can be too permissive. These are people who say things like, "Okay, I'll give you one more chance," after 15 chances already have been given. Consequently, children learn that the rules won't be reinforced and so they learn not to respect the rules.

A balance of consistency and nurturance is required to provide a supportive and predictable environment. Every parent should ask, "What am I weakest in, consistency or nurturance?" Educators can help parents identify their weak points and then parents can begin to work on those aspects.

Children who are experiencing behavior problems often improve when their environment is modified. The following are some home modifications that may be useful.

Useful Home Modifications

Teaching Independence

Nurturing children can be a tricky business. Even though most parents consider children the most precious things on earth, at times it is difficult for them not to make mistakes. Every parent makes mistakes. Problems can arise when a parent who is attempting to nurture his child suffocates him in a blanket of over-protection. Children rely on parents to provide a safe space in which they can explore and become independent beings. Sometimes, though, we mistake a child's attempt to be independent as disrespect. It is important that parents allow their children to develop skills that will help them feel confident and secure. This requires taking the child's lead and going at his pace. It is necessary for parents to give their child the freedom to try new things while recognizing that the mistakes he makes are a way of learning, and an approximation toward a goal.

Role Modeling

Parents demonstrate nurturance to their children by role modeling appropriate ways to express feelings. When a parent makes a mistake he has the opportunity to role model for his child how to correct that mistake: first, by admitting that he made a mistake; second, by apologizing for it and then, rectifying the mistake to the best of his ability.

The affection parents show to their children and to others will have an important impact. Remember that the child may not always hear what the parents are saying, but he most often sees what parents are doing. Finding common ground with a child and sharing human experiences and emotions will teach him how to make his way in the world.

Communication

The way in which a parent communicates also has a great effect on children. Speaking and communicating in a respectful manner teaches the child to do the same. Parents should never talk down to a child. It is essential for the parent to listen when the child is talking and to really hear what he is saying. Providing appropriate feedback in a manner that does not embarrass or humiliate the child will allow him to listen to the parent. A parent must give his child the option to intentionally make mistakes and to take the consequences without a sermon. If the child is too upset to talk about something, the parent needs to give him the time and space he may require to cool down so he can talk rationally. It helps to choose a non-emotional time for a discussion on a difficult issue. There may be times, as well, when the parents will need to do the same for themselves. When the topic is unpleasant for the parent it may be best not to charge on through. No child wants to hear about how badly he is doing or about everything he has done wrong. It is even more difficult to deal with criticism when the child is forced to make eye contact with the adult while being told of his inadequacies. Setting up a situation where eye contact is not required is a good idea.

Parents need to talk with their children at times and places when they are not feeling threatened. Raking leaves, shopping in the mall, and other activities are all suitable times and places for talking with a child about sensitive issues. I had a father of a student tell me that the best time to talk to his son was when he was driving on the highway. He told me, "He doesn't have to look at me, but he sure isn't going anywhere."

Increasing Self-Esteem

Children with behavior problems seem particularly vulnerable to having low self-esteem. The best way to combat this is to start building confidence in children before these negative feelings start. This often can be done at home. Also an educator should encourage parents to get their children involved in activities that increase self-esteem.

Assigning Responsibilities

There are always a million chores to be done at home, and I believe that children with or without behavior problems should have a part in doing them. As in the classroom, chores at home are wonderful for the child with behavior problems. They provide a variety of activities and help make the child feel capable and responsible. A child could do chores such as throwing clothing into a hamper, putting away toys, and carrying dirty dishes to the sink. Other jobs and chores could be discussed with the children at a family meeting.

The parent may or may not decide to give an allowance in return for chores completed. In any event, if the child does jobs or chores above and beyond the call of duty, the parent may want to reward the effort with a special outing, time alone with the parent, or the parent could ask the child what he would like.

Working with Younger or Less-Capable People

Perhaps the most effective responsibility is having a child work with children or adults who could use assistance. This could be beneficial for younger siblings or relatives. Also a child could volunteer at a nursing home, an animal shelter, or any number of other community organizations. Again, like the classroom situation, it is often the child with behavior problems who needs the extra help. Reversing this situation and letting the child know that he is trusted and has something to give, is a terrific confidence booster.

Spending Time with an Older Peer

If there is an older peer, neighbor, or relative a child admires, the educator could suggest that the parent promote a relationship between the two. The parent could encourage the two to spend time together; invite the older child over, or invite him to join the family on an outing. The older child will provide a good role model to the younger, and they both may have a good time! Children with behavior problems can be "turned around" by positive friendships.

Siblings

In most families siblings tend to argue and fight. This problem is sometimes elevated when one or more of the siblings has behavior problems. In the heat of the battle, the child with behavior problems may become totally unreasonable. Parents must teach both the child with behavior problems and the child without how to handle these situations. In most family situations, "the squeaky wheel gets the grease." Children with behavior problems can be very squeaky, and the sibling who does not have behavior problems too often does not get enough attention. Additionally, there will be times when family outings or events have to be altered or canceled because of the disruptive sibling. This can be very difficult for the other sibling who then may begin to harbor resentment and anger at the sibling with behavior problems. Educators can explain to parents that these feelings of anger and resentment should be validated. They are real and reasonable feelings. If the parents can, they should plan some special time with all siblings, both individually and together. Ultimately, how a parent deals with difficult behavior will affect how all children in the family deal with it. For instance, if a parent is a screamer, chances are that one or all of the children in the family will likely become screamers too.

Company and Visitors

If visitors are expected, parents must warn their children so they can adequately prepare. Educators can talk to parents about respecting the child's space at home — space that is important and private. The child may want to put away special items, especially if other children are coming. The educator can instruct the parents on how to help their child organize thoughts to make the preparations. Reminding the child, "The Smiths are coming with their 2-year-old so you may want to put your model airplanes away," is often useful to the child.

The child may get agitated or overly excited if there are children coming over. Unfortunately this may lead to inappropriate behavior that upsets the visiting children. Again, the parents can be instructed to sit down with their child and talk out strategies for a successful visit.

43

Parents can rehearse with their child how to ask others to play, and they can act out possible situations and talk about how to handle the visit.

Preparing the Child for School

Parents should be encouraged to be as communicative with the school as possible. Things will work much better if the parents and the educational staff work together. It is reasonable for parents to request daily or weekly progress reports as appropriate and when the parents have concerns they should be encouraged to let the teacher and school staff know.

There may be times when the parents and the school disagree on certain methods or issues. Sometimes disputes can be serious and even painful. However, it is important for the child to stay out of the "line of fire." The educator needs to help parents understand that if a child gets the message that their parents have no faith in the school or perceive the school staff as not being capable, the child may lose confidence in the school situation. One of the worst things that could happen is an undermining of the structure and limit setting provided at school. In these situations, children with behavior problems learn to manipulate — pitting the school against parent and vice versa. This is a destructive situation where much can be lost. By explaining to the parents that it is vital that they support their child's efforts to be cooperative at school, the educator increases the possibility that school life will be much easier for the child.

Vacations

Vacations can be really difficult for many different reasons. Everyone in the family has expectations of relaxation and good times. This can be devastating because stress and tension usually occur under these situations. For the child with behavior problems, a new schedule, different bedtimes, different food arrangements, and a general feeling of unfamiliar territory are disorienting and confusing. A child returning to school from a vacation that has been filled with frustration and inappropriate behavior will often have behavioral problems that may last for weeks.

Long car trips can be challenging but can be completed without complications. Parents should plan on making frequent stops, and they should bring along games and other activities that can be used in the car.

Bedtime

A common complaint of teachers is that children who do not get enough sleep and come to school tired invariably have behavior problems in school. This is why it is important for educators to assist parents in dealing with bedtime routines and issues. As with almost all aspects of life, consistency is going to be essential for the child with behavior problems. To this end, it is so important for parents to try and have a set bedtime for their child and a set routine before bedtime. It also would be helpful to start doing less stimulating and quieter activities at least one hour before bedtime. Kurcinka (1998) has some wonderful ideas for calming activities that can prepare your child for the upcoming bedtime. These ideas include: running water for a warm bath, dimming the lights, playing tranquil music, back rubbing, reading together, eating a snack, and listening to a story on tape. Kurcinka states that these activities can encourage your child to slow down and switch from active to rest time. "The common factor is that they are soothing and calming and provide solid cues for your child" (p. 202).

Sleeping can be problematic for children with behavior problems. I have heard many parents complain that their children wake up extremely early, and they have asked me for suggestions on how to keep them in bed longer. The answer is, you don't. Parents can set limits for what the child can do when he wakes up early. It would be fine for the child to do art work, watch a video-tape with the volume on low, read a book, or any other quiet activity that will not disturb the other members of the household. Specific rooms can be off limits to them before a certain hour. It is important for parents to teach their child that even though they may be ready to start the day other people in the house may not be ready and that they must respect the needs of others.

Mealtime

As with sleeping, proper nutrition is an important part of a child's life. It has behavioral implications in the educational setting. Many children with behavior problems have problems with eating and mealtime. Mealtimes can be quite troublesome. As a child, I was not always the happiest during mealtime. I felt very confined, and it was a rare meal when I didn't ask to go to the bathroom. I usually was done eating before everyone else and would become frustrated by having to wait at the table with nothing to do. This made me particularly susceptible to being disruptive or to becoming over-reactive to my older sister when she teased me.

Parents need to consider carefully the seating arrangement at the table. They should try not to seat siblings together who do not get along. Establishing specific rules for mealtime can be beneficial, but these rules should be acceptable to everyone.

As with all skills, parenting skills can be learned and, with practice, can improve steadily. Educators should encourage parents and be supportive whenever they can. Parenting is one of the most difficult jobs there is!

47

Chapter Four

Attention Deficit Hyperactivity Disorder

Attention Deficit Hyperactivity Disorder (ADHD) has received quite a bit of scrutiny over the past several years, and much controversy surrounds the over-identification or misdiagnoses of this specific disorder, and the use of medication for treating it.

Identification/Causes

One of the major reasons ADHD is difficult to diagnose is that many of the traits found in children and adults with ADHD are commonly found in people who do not have this disorder or that may have a disorder of some other type. This is sometimes true for individuals that have had a traumatic brain injury or have other events occur in their lives. "It is important to know that ADHD is sometimes mistakenly diagnosed when a child has been exposed to violence and is suffering from posttraumatic stress disorder" (Kaiser and Sklar Raminsky 2003, p. 29). Proper diagnosis is essential for proper placement, treatment, and programming.

There is no perfect method for diagnosing ADHD. "The National Institutes of Health, a most respected federal agency, has stated that there is no such valid test.

49

Most so-called tests are behavior rating scales or questionnaires completed by parents or teachers, or measures of performance such as the ability to pay attention" (Turecki 2000, p. 67). Proper diagnosis, as with other disabilities, involves onset, frequency, and intensity and symptomatic traits.

For the purposes of discussing this topic, an operational definition of ADHD is required. Although each individual will experience different aspects of ADHD and display different types of behaviors, it is important to come to a consistent recognition of what it is and how it is manifested.

There are many different definitions of ADHD. For instance, the *DSM-IV-TR* (2000) diagnostic criteria for ADHD include the following: A child must have either of two sets of symptomatic problems. The first set relates to inattention. At least six of the nine symptomatic problems must have persisted for at least six months to a degree that is maladaptive and inconsistent with a child's developmental level. The nine symptomatic problems are as follows:

> (1) often fails to give close attention to details or makes careless errors in school work or other activities;

> (2) often has difficulty sustaining attention in tasks or play activities;

> (3) often does not seem to listen when spoken to directly;

(4) often does not follow through with instructions and fails to finish schoolwork, chores, or duties in the workplace (not due to oppositional behavior or failure to understand instructions);

(5) often has difficulty organizing tasks and activities;

(6) often avoids, dislikes, or is reluctant to engage in tasks that require sustained mental effort (such as school work or housework);

(7) often loses things necessary for tasks or activities;

(8) is often easily distracted by extraneous stimuli; and

(9) is often forgetful in daily activities.

The second set of symptomatic problems relates to hyperactivity-impulsivity. An individual must demonstrate at least six of nine symptoms and the onset of these symptoms must be no later than 7 years of age and present in at least two or more situations.

(1) often fidgets with hands or feet, or squirming in seat;

(2) often leaves seat in classroom or in other situations in which remaining seated is expected;

51

(3) often runs about or climbs excessively in situations in which it is inappropriate (in adolescents or adults this may be limited to subjective feelings of restlessness);

(4) often has difficulty playing or engaging in leisure activities quietly;

(5) is often "on the go" or often acts as if "driven by a motor;"

(6) often talks excessively;

(7) often blurts out answers before questions have been completed;

(8) often has difficulty awaiting turn; and

(9) often interrupts or intrudes on others (e.g., butts into games or conversations).

ADHD should not be diagnosed if the symptoms can be explained by other medical or psychiatric conditions (e.g., pervasive developmental disorder, schizophrenia, psychotic disorder, or anxiety disorder). Furthermore, children who are emotionally disturbed due to environmental reasons often show the same symptoms as children who have ADHD, and consequently, and unfortunately, these children often are misdiagnosed as having ADHD.

A "commonsense" definition of ADHD can be divided into four broad categories. The first category is "Inattention and Distractibility," which is characterized by difficulty in the following areas: picking appropriate targets for focus, achieving focus, maintaining focus, shifting and dividing focus. The second category is

"Overarousal," which is characterized by excessive restlessness, overactivity, easy arousal, difficulty in controlling body movements, and the display of emotional extremes. The third category, "Impulsivity," is characterized by the following traits: not thinking before acting, not weighing (or identifying consequences of future actions, inability to reasonably consider the consequences or implications of behavior, difficulty with rule-governed behavior). The individual may know certain rules, be able to explain them and give examples, but be unable to control actions and think before acting. The fourth category is "Difficulty with Gratification." Students with ADHD do not work well for long-term rewards. They often require brief, repeated payoffs instead of a single delayed reward, because outcome is critically tied to the frequency, saliency, predictability, and immediacy of the reinforcer (Goldstein 1995).

Although there is no definitive cause, as of yet, for Attention Deficit Hyperactivity Disorder the common consensus is that there may be several causes, and that most likely it is the result of an inherited tendency toward dopamine depletion, or underactivity in those parts of the brain affecting attention, response inhibition and sensitivity to behavioral consequences (Barkley 1990).

A common misconception is that a child can develop ADHD if that child is the product of a chaotic or dysfunctional family. This is simply not true. You cannot "catch" ADHD. Additionally, sugar, food additives and dyes, vitamin deficiencies, lead poisoning, prenatal influences, birth complications, brain damage are not possible causes of this disorder (Barkley 1990). Although these conditions are not a cause, they may, nonetheless, exacerbate a pre-existing condition.

Characteristics: How School Performance and Behavior Are Affected

The hallmark symptoms of ADHD are distractibility, impulsivity, and high activity (Hallowell and Ratey 1994). These features make it difficult for a student to be successful in school. "Many students with Attention Deficit Hyperactivity Disorder can be quite disruptive in class: They fidget; they blurt out answers to questions; they interrupt other students; they lose homework assignments; they flit from one task to another" (Meade 1991, p. 48). "Individuals with Attention Deficit (Hyperactivity Disorder) are usually characterized as having difficulty staying on task, focusing attention, and completing work. In addition, they often display symptoms of age-inappropriate hyperactive behavior, are easily distracted, racing from one idea or interest to another, or produce sloppy and carelessly done work. They impart the impression that they are not listening or have not heard what they have been told" (Lerner and Lerner 1991, p. 1). It is manifested by some of the following symptoms: difficulty waiting turn; interruptions, blurting out answers to questions; difficulty playing quietly; leaving seat often; running or climbing excessively; fidgeting; excessive talking; inability to remain still; difficulty following through on instructions; difficulty sustaining attention; losing things necessary for tasks; failing to give close attention to details; disorganization; making careless mistakes; forgetfulness; daydreaming; lack of motivation to complete school work and tasks (Aust 1994).

Once identified and diagnosed, students with ADHD have the ability to charm the socks off educational staff people or to infuriate them to tears. The "come and go" and "ebb and flow" nature of the disorder often has teachers believing that these students are picking and choosing times to act out. Yet, for many of these students school is a nightmare.

* * * * * * * *

Case History

Jenny is one such student. Jenny just finished fifth-grade in a public elementary school. She is a pretty young girl whose eyes sparkle. She is capable and bright, but has had difficulty in school. Jenny is classified by the committee on special education. She is in a regular education program with modifications built into her schedule, and she receives consultant teacher services.

Jenny's problems in school began to surface in second-grade. She was diagnosed with ADHD by a neurologist. Her school history includes inappropriate behavior such as outbursts, screaming, yelling, crying, leaving the room without permission, and hiding under her desk. Jenny's mother described her as being "very immature" and said she "can get physically aggressive."

This past school year was a particularly difficult year for her. She experienced quite a bit of frustration and displayed recurring inappropriate behavior. Although both Jenny and her mother acknowledged that her behavior did not change from home to school, Jenny's mother felt her difficulties in school were partly due to a teacher who just did not know how to handle her daughter. Jenny's mother acknowledged that her daughter has had some wonderful teachers, but felt that when teachers don't understand what the problem is and how to deal with it, everyone suffers —

Every day that I stand there with her at the bus stop . . . I feel like I'm sending her off to a torture chamber because of what she has to experience with teachers . . . teachers who don't understand, and teachers who torment her . . . and the classmates who torment her as a result of "the look." You know the teacher doesn't have to say anything. The roll of the eyes, the body language tells every student in the class that this child is nothing but a pain in my butt, and I don't understand why she can't just behave. My biggest gripe is the fact that many of the general mainstream teachers don't understand these children at all. And not that they need to be experts, but if they could just simply be exposed to what makes these children tick and what makes these children not tick. If they could just understand what this kid is going through. This kid is not trying to be bad. They just have these impulsive actions that just drive everybody crazy. You know, they'll be in a class discussion and finally Jenny will raise her hand and the teacher will go "Jenny what is the answer?" and Jenny will say, "Can I go to the bathroom?" and you just want to rip her little head off. I can understand the teacher's frustration, but in a heated discussion that is what she is going to say. She is not going to give you the answer. That's not why she is raising her hand.

. . .

She's thinking outside the box and the rest of us are thinking inside the box.

A common complaint of teachers is that students with ADHD do not have the necessary social skills for school success. Very often they are referred to as socially incompetent and immature. It seems that these students act about one-third less mature than their peers. Thus, a 6-year-old acts like a 4-year-old; a 12-year-old acts like an 8-year-old and a 15-year-old acts like a 10-year-old.

"Many children with Attention Deficit Hyperactivity Disorder have serious interpersonal difficulties and experience peer rejection. Although not all children with [this disorder] have social skills deficits, it is a problem for many" (Lerner and Lerner 1991, p. 15).

Jenny had few friends, according to her mother —

She doesn't get invited to too many parties. Her younger sister gets invited to every-

thing. Jenny once said to me, 'You know, Mommy, I used to think that I didn't want to play with any of the kids. I used to say I don't care, but I did care. I was so lonely for friends.'

There can be significant aggressive and antisocial behaviors associated with this behavior disorder. Between 30 percent to 90 percent of children diagnosed with ADHD have significant conduct problems (Frick and Lahey 1991). Jenny's mother described such an incident —

A kid pushed her. She had a brand new blouse on that we had just bought her. After she was pushed she fell into her art project, and I had told her earlier, 'Don't get your blouse dirty.' After she fell into her project, she got marker all over her blouse and it wasn't coming off. Then she just lost it. She turned around and grabbed the kid, threw him on the table and started flipping tables over. There were projects everywhere and then she just got on top of this kid and just pounded him.

In addition to antisocial characteristics, many students with ADHD also have low self-esteem and very little confidence. They are so easily frustrated and give up quickly when a task is too challenging. They usually perform better when given individual instruction. The issues of self-esteem, however, are always there, even when there is individual attention.

Attention Deficit Hyperactivity Disorder

Jenny takes private piano lessons. In this setting, Jenny has one-on-one instruction from a music teacher. Jenny's music instructor, Stacey Srulowitz, who is a certified teacher with more than 10 years of public school teaching experience, reported —

> *She [Jenny] is a good student. She does practice. She has difficulty when she makes mistakes. She has a very low threshold for frustration. She gets very upset and says she can't do it and wants to give up. She will get so frustrated, at times, that I'll see tears in her eyes. Her lack of confidence doesn't allow her to expand. She has a problem fulfilling her potential because of her own frustration. I feel that her potential is very great, and I feel that she is very, very bright.*

Sometimes medication can help reduce those symptoms that contribute to feelings of low self-esteem and frustration. Such was the case with Jenny, according to her mother —

> *It's difficult because she knows she's different. She's on Paxil. We chemically make her feel better about herself because she's got to have something. She knows she's smart. She knows she has a lot of talent and stuff.*

In some cases students with ADHD become experts in figuring out how to gain something they need, which may

© 2007 LRP Publications; all rights reserved.   **59**

reduce or satisfy the frustration levels they feel. Jenny's mother put it this way —

> *When Jenny says you're so pretty, it's just so that she can get something from you. It's not because she really thinks you are.*

Many individuals with ADHD are sensitive. Their feelings are easily hurt. Or they are sympathetic and sometimes see themselves as the "defenders of the downtrodden." Jenny's music teacher describes her this way —

> *Jenny is one of the most compassionate children I have ever met. I believe she is very sensitive. Whenever I tell her something bad, she always wants to make me feel better. She's an amazing child.*

Unfortunately, sometimes they also can be quite insensitive. It is not uncommon for a student with ADHD to point out something embarrassing about another person in a very public place with a very loud voice, or to impulsively perform an act without thinking. According to her mother, Jenny displays this behavior characteristic —

> *She is kind-hearted when it comes to little children and creatures that might be injured . . . and then on the other hand she might decide to dissect a frog with the edge of a rock. Whatever crosses her mind comes out on the lips. And you just can't*

> *take it personally, but that's just what hap-*
> *pens with some teachers.*

Jenny's mother described a particular incident that occurred in school that was quite upsetting to both her and her daughter —

> *Jenny was in school one day and she hadn't*
> *done her work. The teacher sent her out of*
> *the room. So, while she was outside the*
> *room, the teacher engaged all the children*
> *in a conversation about what it is that*
> *bothers them about Jenny. They put a list*
> *up on the board. She then called Jenny*
> *back into the class, and the teacher went*
> *down the list in front of the class with*
> *Jenny just standing there.*

Jenny's mother realized that the teacher thought this was a good intervention for her daughter, but she felt that it only ended up having a devastating effect on her.

> *They had to call in the school psychologist*
> *because Jenny threatened to kill herself.*
> *There were days this year that when I sent*
> *Jenny to school her quietness was so quiet*
> *that I would call the school to see if she*
> *actually walked in the door.*

Jenny's response to this particular incident —

> *I hate my teacher. She wrote a list of things*
> *that she hates about me. She's a witch. I*
> *like all the other teachers.*

* * * * * * * *

Strategies

Every student is an individual including students who have Attention Deficit Hyperactivity Disorder. It would be a mistake to believe that all students identified as having ADHD display the same types of behaviors. I have known ADHD students who have been loud and disruptive, and I have known students who have been quiet and withdrawn. Dealing with students, no matter what the behavior, takes patience, firmness, and kindness.

The type of behavior management program used with students who have ADHD is the key to successful academic and behavioral programming. "It is essential to remember to avoid punitive measures and permissive approaches; these result in power struggles that are ineffective, waste time, and damage the relationship between the teacher and student" (Boynton and Boynton 2005, p. 154).

There should be a multidisciplinary and multimodal treatment plan in place that should be maintained for a long period of time (Goldstein 1990; Barkley 1990). By far, the most effective interventions for ADHD children and adolescents in the classroom reflect the use of behavioral techniques and medicine (Goldstein 1990).

Behavioral approaches represent a broad set of specific interventions that have the common goal of modifying the physical and social environment to alter or change behavior (AAP 2001).

Medication

Medication often becomes a source of friction in the school environment. Some parents feel that school staff want their children on medication in order to make the teacher's life easier. Unfortunately, because so many children have been prescribed medication (appropriately and inappropriately) there is a heightened sensitivity toward it. Ultimately, the decision about its use is up to the parents. Hopefully, this decision is made after careful consideration of the individual student and a thorough medical evaluation. When, however, a student with ADHD is having a difficult time in school, and medication has been recommended by a physician so that the student can function effectively and, more importantly, feel better, I would surely recommend at least a trial use of the medication. Medication does not "fix the problem," it can, however, help individuals utilize resources to the best of their abilities.

"The medication works like a pair of eyeglasses, helping the individual to focus. It can also reduce the sense of inner turmoil and anxiety that is so common with Attention Deficit Hyperactivity Disorder" (Hallowell and Ratey 1994, p. 20). I often explain to parents that medication can help children access their education.

Jenny's mother spoke about her decision to give her daughter medication. She explained that her first attempts to change Jenny's difficult behavior involved changing Jenny's environment —

> We went back to church. We had her go to
> karate. We had her on a special diet . . . no

63

additives no preservatives. This was done to correct her behavior, but it didn't.

After diagnosis Jenny was immediately put on the medicine and that was at the time when everybody was saying, "Oh, what are you doing? The teachers are lazy; the parents are lazy." There was something so wrong with her that I knew I had to do something. It made me feel a little bit bad, but I couldn't live with the way it was. It was really tough for her and then the first day I gave her the Ritalin I sent her to school. This is a kid that tells me nothing and she came home from school that day and I said, "How was school today?" She sat there and her eyes welled up with tears, and she looked at me and she said, "I don't know what, Mom, but today I could concentrate. There wasn't all this noise going on in my head, and when the teacher was talking I could focus on what she was saying" . . . and the tears are coming down her face.

Rachel Warren, a public school teacher with 25 years of teaching experience has worked in an alternative public school, an ungraded school, and in a traditional public school. Warren often is against the use of medication and feels that changing the environment of the classroom and individualizing a program for a student is the best answer. However, she concedes that sometimes changing the environment is not enough and cautions that when a student is placed on medication it is important that the dosage is accurate and to also consider other factors. She experienced this with one particular student in her class —

> *Before Donny took medication he was difficult to manage if not impossible. He did a lot of running around and hiding under tables. He couldn't follow directions. He was sometimes mean to the classroom animals. If you gave him a piece of paper, he might tear it up. He was very impatient. If you could get him to stay still, he liked hugging. So he was at times, likable. We weren't sure we could keep him in school. Then he started taking Ritalin. In the beginning, on the medication, he was too quiet and withdrawn. I think he was getting too much medication. It had to be adjusted. It took about six months before the dosage was correct. Once he was on the medication, we discovered he was smart and that he could really do his work. Without the medication, we didn't know what his abilities were. He appeared to be without skills . . . you know reading and writing. He even appeared to be mildly retarded. With medication, he began to learn and he began to write. After he was on medication, Donny became an excellent math student. Doing math seemed to calm him down. However, even with the medication, he still didn't*

65

> *have friends. Our class was different. Our kids had individualized lesson plans. Donny's assignments were individualized so that they could be totally appropriate for him. It was time-consuming and hard to do but it paid off. It was exciting.*

Medication is not always the answer. There are many parents who have reported that their child suffered from side effects of medication. It is essential that you work closely with a physician who has a thorough knowledge of ADHD. If a child is on medication, that child should be monitored regularly. Also, keep in mind, that medication alone does not usually work; a student requires other supports to be successful in school. Ultimately, students need to learn how to monitor their behavior.

"The treatment of ADHD (whether behavioral, pharmacological, or multimodal) requires the development of child-specific treatment plans that describe not only the methods and goals of treatment, but also include means of monitoring over time and specific plans for follow-up. The process of developing target out comes requires careful input from parent, children and teachers as well as other school personnel where available and appropriate" (U.S. Office of Special Education Programs 2003, p.13).

Structure and Consistency

Structure and consistency are important for all students, but vital for ADHD students. Limits need to be set and consequences applied. Once structure and consistency are built into a program, follow-through is essential. Consequences should be delivered in a calm and swift manner.

Provision of close supervision during unstructured times, like recess, is necessary to help control impulsive and risk-taking behavior (Meade 1996).

Useful strategies in dealing with disruptive behavior may include: frequent verbal feedback, classroom token economies, home-school contingencies that combine the efforts of school and parents to improve children's classroom behavior, and peer-mediated interventions that draw upon classmates of the student with Attention Deficit Hyperactivity Disorder to share feedback in an appropriate manner (Lerner and Lerner 1991). (Behavior modification programs are presented in Chapter Eleven.)

"A number of general suggestions can be extrapolated from the available research literature. Classrooms for inattentive children should be organized and structured, with clear rules, predictable schedules, and separate desks. Feedback and rewards should be consistent, immediate, and frequent. A response cost reinforcement program is recommended as an integral part of the classroom, but minor disruptions that do not bother others should be ignored. Academic material should be matched to the child's ability, and tasks should vary but be generally interesting to the child. Transition times, as well as recess and assemblies, should be closely supervised. Teachers and parents, especially in the lower school years, should maintain close communication. Teacher expectations should be adjusted to meet the child's skill level, both behaviorally and academically. Finally, teachers must be educated concerning the issues of Attention Deficit Hyperactivity Disorder in the classroom and helped to develop a repertoire of behavioral interventions that mini-

67

mize the negative impact of the child's temperament, both on that child and on the entire classroom population" (Goldstein 1995, p. 76).

Summary — Issues and Suggestions

As previously mentioned, the ultimate goal is to teach students with ADHD how to monitor their behavior. Cognitive training is an excellent way to do so. "The central goal of cognitive training for children with ADHD is the development of self-control skills and reflective problem-solving strategies, both of which are presumed to be deficient in children with this disorder" (Lerner and Lerner 1991, p. 13). Cognitive training involves the development of metacognitve skills that can be quite useful in problem-solving. (This type of training involves teaching the student to think about thinking and is reviewed in Chapter Eleven.)

Self-esteem issues need to be addressed. (Techniques for improving self-esteem are outlined in Chapter Eleven.) Constant encouragement and support are required. "The person with Attention Deficit Hyperactivity Disorder benefits from a 'coach'; someone standing on the sidelines with a whistle around his neck calling out encouragement, instructions, and reminders, and in general helping to keep things going on task" (Hallowell and Ratey 1994, p. 20). This can be tiresome, but the benefits usually are worth it.

Another issue, changes in routine, can be particularly problematic for students with ADHD. Public school teacher, Rachel Warren, described her method of dealing with potential problems during a class assembly —

> *If a child is disruptive, I might have them sit on my lap . . . little ones. If there was a teacher who could watch my class, I might take them out of the assembly to talk to them. If I felt that they were upset before the assembly and I anticipated that the assembly would be hard for them, I might not bring them. I might bring them to the library or some other safe place.*

Jenny's mother described what Jenny's school provided for her —

> *They have a special aide. They have a school psychologist. They have a constant open-door policy with the school psychologist. Anytime Jenny wants to go in there, if she wants to keep going, she can. She gets counseling in school. The school would do whatever they could to try and figure out what they could do for her. Many of the teachers were patient with her. They gave her wide margins.*

Jenny's music teacher added —

> *I think the best thing you can do for a kid with ADHD is to give him reassurance constantly, and no matter what mistake it's all right . . . and just be as patient and as positive as you can be.*

Warren provides the following for ADHD students even when dealing with 28 other students in her class —

I allow those kids to move around. They can do hands-on activities. If a child can't follow directions I ask him to do something else in another part of the room, and I might assign someone to help him with it. I might have a class meeting to discuss behavior. What helps kids with Attention Deficit Hyperactivity Disorder is to find out what their interests are. I think it helps a lot. If you're going to go for their interests, you're going to get their attention. It helps a great deal to have a relationship with kids with this disorder so that they learn to trust you. I think the classroom environment has a lot to do with success. In my class, the kids would not be asked to sit for very long periods of time. Another thing is that the kids would be allowed to talk. I don't mean yelling and fooling around. I don't mean anything chaotic. They'd be allowed to talk quietly with other kids. They wouldn't have to be silent. They would have to be quiet only when lessons were going on. An important thing is that they would have to respect not just the teacher, but the other kids also. It's crucial that the teacher involve the other students in helping the kid who can't pay attention. Being too authoritative doesn't work. Put-

ting them down doesn't work or comparing them to other kids doesn't work.

As Jenny's music teacher addressed the issue —

I constantly give her reinforcement and I think I have a good rapport with her. I think she would be upset with herself if she caused me to get angry with her.

Another issue to recognize is the added stress in dealing with a child with ADHD, not only in school, but also at home. Stress often exacerbates behavioral problems in both environments. Both the child and the family members may benefit from family counseling to help repair injured self-esteem, overcome feelings of demoralization or depression, or learn more effective behavioral approaches (Lerner and Lerner 1991). Social skills and cognitive training also can be conducted in counseling sessions.

Most important, parents should listen to their child and teachers should listen to their students. Only they truly understand what they feel, what they need, and what you should know. The following Question and Answer forum with Jenny attests to that.

* * * * * * * *

Q. What do you think makes a good teacher?

A. Someone who doesn't get mad when you need help. And after they give the directions up on the board they don't mind if someone says, "Could you come here? I don't understand . . ." and doesn't pick a favorite in class.

This last teacher picked on me. All the other ones were nice.

Q. What's easy or fun in school?

A. Art.

Q. Do you prefer to do things where you can move around and draw?

A. Yeah. I like science. I like things that go boom.

Q. Do you do better when you have something to do in your hands or when you don't have something in yours hands?

A. When I have something to do with my hands.

Q. Do you have trouble sitting still?

A. Yeah. I'm always wiggling and doodling.

Q. What's the hardest thing about school? What do you have difficulty doing?

A. Paying attention. I have trouble staying on the subject.

Q. What makes you mad in school?

A. When the teacher assigns something that I don't really understand and I need help, but she says, "I don't want to explain it again."

Q. What about homework?

A. Well, some of the homework I do and some of the homework I don't.

Q. What happens when you don't do your homework?

A. Mom gets mad at me.

Q. Does that help you to get your work done?

A. No.

Q. If you were the teacher and you had a kid who had Attention Deficit Disorder what would you do for that kid?

A. I'd give her more attention. Like, I'd make everything a more narrow path to follow. But still do it so you're not showing that you're doing it for them, for that one kid.

Q. Do you sometimes think that you stick out in school?

A. Yeah.

Q. How does that make you feel?

A. Sad.

Q. Do you like when you have one-to-one assistance? Like when you have a teacher help you?

A. No! Too much attention.

Q. What should I tell teachers to do for kids like you?

A. I would tell them not to be so brief and be so general, and tell them exactly and not to be so general in the subject.

73

Attention Deficit Hyperactivity Disorder

Attention Deficit Hyperactivity Disorder (ADHD) is a disorder characterized by difficulties with attention and activity.

Characteristics:

- Hyperactivity

- Attention problems

- Distractibility/impulsivity

- Immaturity

- Learning difficulties

- Low-tolerance of frustration

- Lack of self-esteem

- Emotionally volatile (not always)

- Oppositional behavior defiance (not always)

Treatment/Intervention:

- Regular and organized routine

- Provisions of modifications

- Role play social situations

- Set clear limits and follow through

- Pre-setting

- Structure
- Consistency
- Teach multiple solution generation
- Behavior modification
- Metacognition
- External scaffolding
- Social skills training
- Self-esteem enhancement
- Medication

75

Chapter Five

Fetal Alcohol Syndrome

Students who have Fetal Alcohol Syndrome face innumerable academic and social difficulties. It is a disorder that is totally preventable, but unfortunately, a disorder with which many students have to deal.

Identification/Causes

Fetal Alcohol Syndrome is a birth defect caused by prenatal exposure to alcohol. This syndrome is diagnosed after identification of growth deficiency (prenatally or postnatally, for height or weight, or both), a specific pattern of minor anomalies that includes a characteristic face (eye slits, flat midface, short upturned nose, ridges running between the nose and the lips, a thin upper lip), and some central nervous system damage that might include microcephaly (small brain size), tremors, hyperactivity, fine or gross motor problems, attentional deficits, learning disabilities, cognitive impairments or developmental delays (Streissguth 1999, p. 22).

"Alcohol, a legal substance, is responsible for much more damage to unborn babies than any legal drug. Drinking during pregnancy — especially heavy or binge drinking — causes lifelong damage to the developing brain, and consuming even small amounts of alcohol can cause

77

neurological deficits" (Kaiser and Sklar Raminsky 2003, p. 30).

It sometimes is difficult to identify an individual with Fetal Alcohol Syndrome because not everyone who has the disorder has discernible physical characteristics. Learning difficulties and disruptive behavior can be incorrectly attributed to other causes. As a result, many students affected do not receive correct diagnosis or treatment for their alcohol-related disabilities (Stratton, Howe and Battaglia 1996). Additionally, biological mothers do not always readily divulge information concerning the fact that they drank alcohol while they were pregnant. It usually is within the educational system that children with Fetal Alcohol Syndrome are identified, due to the developmental or physical problems these children display (Williams, Howard and McLaughlin 1994).

A diagnosis of this disorder only is accurate after a clinical examination. At this time, however, there are no confirming laboratory tests and no validated checklists (Streissguth 1999). A diagnosis is warranted when a child has a cluster of the aforementioned disorders within three diagnostic areas: central nervous system dysfunction, craniofacial malformations, and prenatal/postnatal development (Griesbach and Polloway 1990).

The diagnosis of Fetal Alcohol Syndrome relies on a composite of specific physical, psychological, and behavioral tests. Specific programs or services for the individual and caregiver are required for accurate diagnosis and appropriate long-term management (Alberta Partnership on Fetal Alcohol Syndrome 2000).

Sally O'Connor, an educator for 10 years, is a special education consultant teacher. She has worked with approximately 25 students who have been diagnosed with Fetal Alcohol Syndrome and were between the ages of 12 and 19. As an educator, O'Connor has been frustrated by inadequate identification of students with this disorder —

> *I'd like to see a better screening process for Fetal Alcohol Syndrome. I think Fetal Alcohol often goes undiagnosed. I see kids that I would swear have it. They have the facial features, behaviors, and cognitive deficits, yet they are unidentified and undiagnosed.*

Characteristics: How School Performance and Behavior Are Affected

There are several school problems associated with Fetal Alcohol Syndrome. Difficult behavior is, perhaps, the most serious of these problems. "The primary challenge that children with Fetal Alcohol Syndrome present at school is their disruptive, unpredictable, or uninterpretable behavior" (Streissguth 1999, p. 208). Children with Fetal Alcohol Syndrome are often impulsive. They "have a problem with impulse control because prenatal exposure to alcohol damages the frontal lobe, which controls inhibitions and judgment" (Kaiser and Sklar Raminsky 2003, p. 143).

The biological effects are exacerbated if the home environment is dysfunctional. If the child with this disorder still lives with the birth mother and/or father, and the parents continue to abuse alcohol, it is not surprising that the child's problems will increase.

According to O'Connor —

> *My personal view of Fetal Alcohol Syndrome is that there are two aspects. There is the physical aspect of what the child is born with and the environmental aspect for those children whose mothers don't stop drinking after they are born. I think that the greater damage is from the environmental factors. I think that's where many of these behaviors come from. Many times I've heard these students say things like, "my mom doesn't care about me." Many times when I have tried to contact parents I have a difficult time getting a hold of them. Either they don't return my phone calls or they'll even be unaware of what school their child goes to. They seem very disinterested in what their child is doing.*

Eileen Gallagher was a special education teacher for six years. She also has worked as a trainer collaborating with teachers on special education issues and as a special education coordinator. According to Gallagher, she has observed specific features and behavior patterns in those students she worked with at the elementary level who had Fetal Alcohol Syndrome —

> *There were several features that really seemed to stand out significantly with the students I worked with. They seemed to*

have an inability to concentrate. They also seemed to become easily irritated by their peers. During less-structured activities their tolerance for being near other kids or having other kids interact with them beyond a very routinized activity was very, very low. There was also an issue about lack of recognition of cause and effect. An "if . . . then" scenario had no impact on them. They didn't generalize information. Day after day they would make the same mistakes over and over again. Out on the playground, reminding them to not do something dangerous on the monkey bars would have no effect the next day . . . even if they had been hurt the day before. They would see something or have an impulse to run across the parking lot and dart out between the school buses.

O'Connor noticed similar patterns of behavior in those students with whom she had worked —

These students engaged in physical aggression . . . fighting, passive aggression . . . refusing to do work. There was also lots of verbal arguing with teachers . . . arguing with classmates . . . calling out, getting into trouble with other students. I often found these students would sometimes withdraw completely. That happened especially when

81

*the students felt that the cognitive tasks
were over their heads.*

As O'Connor and Gallagher pointed out, the neurological and cognitive problems associated with this disorder are directly related to the difficulties these students have with behavior. "The basic cognitive, attention, and memory problems of children and adolescents with Fetal Alcohol Syndrome set the stage for behavior problems in the classroom because of repeated failure to meet expectations. Basic communication problems and difficulty with self-reflection make verbal communication of needs difficult" (Streissguth 1999, p. 135). Additionally, students often cannot describe clearly what is happening to them. Their responses reveal their lack of comprehension.

O'Connor acknowledged that many of the children with whom she worked had processing difficulties that impeded social growth. Processing problems also contributed to issues of mistrust —

> *The major problem that these students have is mistrust of authority. One way or another that's what it always comes down to being. These students have not just verbal language processing problems, but physical language processing problems as well. Posturing or coming close to them is often misunderstood. Interpreting social gestures and interpreting verbal information definitely plays into not trusting adults. Even in non-threatening situations*

there is lack of eye contact, arms crossed . . .
simply because that person is an adult.

Gallagher observed similar processing difficulties her students seemed to have —

> They could complete a simple academic task in one day and be unable to do the same task one day later. They would know that they had seen it before, but they couldn't do it. I think they became frustrated because they couldn't process it completely. I think frustration, from feeling like they knew, they should know, or that they used to know, was caused by processing deficits. I think this made them irritable and oppositional. That's when they tear up their paper and throw it across the room. Sometimes they appear oppositional because of those processing deficits. They don't want to be bad. They just don't get it. These were darling children who had processing issues that prevented them from participating socially and academically.

Other behavior problems of students with Fetal Alcohol Syndrome may include: failure to consider the consequences of actions, a lack of appropriate initiative, unresponsiveness to subtle facial cues, and a lack of reciprocal friendships with peers (Williams, Howard and McLaughlin 1994). More specifically, behavior problems include difficulties in modulating incoming stimuli (Streissguth 1999). This is evidenced by overstimulation in social situations, strong emotional overreaction to situations, displays of rapid mood swings that occur after small events, poor attention span, difficulty completing tasks and the tendency to misplace things. "The bright-eyed manner that belies their cognitive impairments makes children with Fetal Alcohol Syndrome especially vulnerable to the vicissitudes of life at school" (Streissguth 1999, p. 134).

These students often appear to be purposely oppositional. Difficulties with compliance, however, may occur due to impediments beyond their control. "Problems with attention, distraction, and memory can interfere with children's successful compliance with adult requests, no matter how hard the children want to please" (Streissguth 1999, p. 134). Unfortunately, for some students, their inability to comprehend the requests and demands in the classroom can cause oppositional behavior. At times this may be interpreted as willful disobedience. In reality, as Gallagher stated, many of these students seek out teacher approval. They do not wish to misbehave. "They are often highly motivated to please teachers they like but may have difficulty relating to teachers who don't give clear commands, say too many things at once, or are inconsistent even though friendly and effusive" (Streissguth 1999, p. 209).

They also have difficulty in social situations due to poor cause-and-effect reasoning (Streissguth 1999). These students seem unaware of the consequences of their behavior, show poor judgment in whom to trust, interrupt with poor timing, do not understand subtle hints, and crave and seek attention. They have few friends and are vulnerable to being taken advantage of by classmates.

O'Connor pointed out that her students would use poor judgment in choosing the few friends they did have —

> *These students tend to hang out with other kids who get into trouble, kids who are causing a lot of disruption in the class-room. Even if they're not doing it them-selves, [the disrupting], they like to see it.*

As previously mentioned, students with Fetal Alcohol Syndrome find it difficult to deal with multiple-sensory inputs, particularly auditory information (Stratton, Howe and Battaglia 1996). Gallagher recalled a young boy who experienced difficulty with noise —

> *One of the boys I worked with who had Fetal Alcohol Syndrome was particularly sensitive to noise. He would almost shriek and run out of the room if it was too noisy for him.*

"These students are often sensitive to perceived slights and do not respond well to embarrassment or condescension. Feelings of resentment for perceived inconsistencies or unfairness can trigger bizarre behaviors" (Streissguth 1999, p. 220). O'Connor said her students would spend a great deal of time trying to protect themselves in social situations —

> *Children with Fetal Alcohol Syndrome are very unintentionally self-centered. They are not conscious of the fact that they're*

85

self-centered. They are very focused on protecting themselves, getting their needs met and making sure that others don't take away things that they need. They can be very territorial. Mostly, it's "me, me, me." I think they have trouble getting close to others because they are so focused on getting their own needs met and helping themselves. Sometimes it's because no one has been there for them, particularly if their parents are still abusing alcohol and are neglectful.

Additional problems that can contribute to inappropriate behavior may include hyperactivity, poor hand-eye coordination, attentional impairments, learning disabilities, deficits in higher order receptive and expressive language, poor impulse control, memory impairments, difficulties with judgment, difficulties with abstract reasoning and poor adaptive functioning (Streissguth 1999). Other symptoms include motor dysfunction (slow performance time, weak grasp, difficulty with hand-eye coordination, tremors, and motor incoordination) and developmental delay (mental impairment and language disability) (Williams, Howard and McLaughlin, 1994). Individuals with Fetal Alcohol Syndrome often are overwhelmed by stimulation and unable to either respond appropriately or protect themselves from the overstimulation of competing ambiguous demands (Streissguth 1999).

As the students get older, O'Connor said, they try to mask their disabilities from their peers in an attempt to reduce their "differentness" in order to fit in —

> *Establishing trust is the hardest thing, especially at the high school level. They don't want to stick out when they're older, and they start rejecting modifications designed for them. "I can handle this all by myself" is the attitude. They don't want to look different.*

Ariana Lowenthal has been a school psychologist for more than 30 years in an inner city school district. She also has served as the chairwoman on the district's city-wide Committee on Special Education. Throughout her career, Lowenthal has worked with students with various behavior problems, yet, she said, it was difficult to determine which students had Fetal Alcohol Syndrome. Like O'Connor, Lowenthal suspected that many students had this disorder but were not diagnosed.

★ ★ ★ ★ ★ ★ ★ ★

Case History No. 1

Richard was diagnosed by a neurologist as having Fetal Alcohol Syndrome. His mother was a single parent who had a history of alcoholism. Lowenthal first started to work with Richard when he was in kindergarten. She noticed Richard had the specific facial features that were consistent for students with this disorder and that he displayed its unique behavior patterns —

When Richard started in kindergarten he was just wild . . . berserk . . . just out of control. He ran out of the room, out of the building onto busy streets. The principal had to chase after him and stay in the classroom to keep him safe. It was really frightening. In the room, he ran about seeming not to know what to do, very disorganized. He wasn't screaming for his mother or screaming "I don't want to go to school." He seemed to have no notion of how to play or what to do with toys. He couldn't follow directions and could not be contained in the kindergarten classroom. There were certain things he could do really well. He could speak well, and when settled down in a one-to-one situation, he could converse with, and relate appropriately to, the other person. His behavior was not defiant; he was just out of his element.

He had very wide-set eyes, very flat nose. The space from his nose to his top lip was very long. He was a little odd-looking, but he was cute.

Physically he had tremendous problems with perceptual motor skills and spatial relations. He was clumsy and could not copy forms or letters. In a large group he seemed to have some problems with audi-

tory processing and often was confused about what the teacher was saying and expecting the children to do.

Working with Richard's mother was an important aspect of his programming. Lowenthal and the school district worked with her on learning parenting skills and in accepting responsibility for her alcoholism and its consequences —

> *Richard's mother was actively drinking . . . denying that she drank. Sometimes I would have to get Richard from home to bring him to school. His mother couldn't get up to get him to the school bus. She was drunk. Sometimes Richard would come to school without the proper clothes. When the mother found out that Richard had Fetal Alcohol Syndrome and that it was caused by her drinking, she was devastated. Eventually the mother started to admit that she was drinking and began to go to Alcoholics Anonymous. Once she did that, she began to feel guilty about her drinking and what it did to her children. We had a social worker working with the mother to help her take care of the kids better, like getting them dressed and so on. The mother actually loved her children very much, whether she was drinking or not. It's just that she wasn't available to them when she was drinking.*

Due to the difficulties Richard was having, special curricular and program modifications were put into place, Lowenthal explained —

> *Our first-step was to have Richard go to the resource room for most of the kindergarten session. In that very small, confined group he learned to play with toys and to interact calmly with peers. Gradually he was able to join the larger group for longer periods. He responded well to structure and familiarity. During his primary school years, he spent up to half the day in the resource room. Writing and math were a challenge for him, and he progressed slowly in these areas. His ability to read was pretty much at grade level and he participated in regular reading groups. As comprehension and analytical skills increased in difficulty after second-grade, he required much more support. His IQ was only about 80 with strengths in vocabulary and weaknesses in visual-motor and analytical skills. After third-grade, he joined a special education class for academic instruction. His social skills had progressed well enough to allow him to participate in a regular class for some part of each day.*

Dealing emotionally with Fetal Alcohol Syndrome can be difficult for children. After Richard found out he had this disorder, he began experiencing different feelings—

> *In the fourth- or fifth-grade Richard went through a period of being withdrawn, of not participating in activities, failing to complete assignments, of not wanting to go to regular class. He seemed depressed. The social worker asked him what was going on. He said, "I hate myself. I hate the way I look, I wish I was dead." The social worker told him he looked fine to her, but he insisted his face was, "like this because my mother drinks." He did respond to counseling and regained his equilibrium.*

Although Richard never seemed to progress above a third-grade level, Lowenthal said, he made gains in his socialization skills —

> *Once he got familiar with the environment, he was not as much of a behavior problem. By the time Richard was 10, he had reached a level of organization that allowed him to participate in many school activities independently and enjoy social interactions. He just did not learn well academically and seemed stuck at the second- and third-grade level. His peers, however, liked him. He was cooperative and a good citizen in school.*

91

* * * * * * * *

Strategies

One of the most important strategies in dealing with Fetal Alcohol Syndrome is early detection so that treatment can begin as soon as possible. "It is important to recognize that although children are affected by prenatal exposure to alcohol, a great deal of neurological development occurs postnatally, and if child care, nutrition, and environment are adequate, it is probable that alcohol-exposed children can make considerable progress. This is particularly true if the insult has not been severe" (Stratton, Howe and Battaglia 1996).

Alcohol abuse, particularly during pregnancy, generally is unacceptable in our society. This viewpoint can have a negative effect on the way students with Fetal Alcohol Syndrome are perceived. Due to attitudes related to alcohol abuse, it is important for educators who deal with students who are the product of alcohol abuse to treat the child as an individual and not a diagnosis (Stratton, Howe and Battaglia 1996). These students need love and hold high expectations. "The students should be made to feel they are an integral and important part of the local school family; this can be accomplished through mainstreaming and reverse mainstreaming. In other words, these special children should be loved and respected so that their self-esteem grows and facilitates their acceptance in American society" (Shelton and Cook 1993, p. 46).

Taking into account the individual needs of students with this disorder is essential. They don't all exhibit the same behavioral or cognitive difficulties. It is important to understand why these students act out. According to O'Connor —

I found the best thing to do is to find out what they're hoping to gain by their inappropriate behavior. Sometimes they act out to avoid attention; sometimes it's to get attention. Every student with Fetal Alcohol Syndrome is different.

Since many students with this disorder have communication problems, they frequently are misunderstood. The frustration this causes is a trigger for them to engage in challenging behavior. "It is essential to provide opportunities for the student to communicate and then to honor those attempts. Although time-consuming at first, we must help the student to build trust in the fact that his or her communications have meaning. After that trust has been established, we can slowly and systematically build delays by asking the child to wait before we honor his or her request" (Burgess and Streissguth 1992, p. 26).

In order to successfully complete tasks, these students need constant reminders, a longer than anticipated training period, and various systems of sequencing and organizing. Additionally, for social success, they need to have positive experiences, develop strategies to maintain emotional control, learn to recognize and communicate their needs, and become aware of cause and effect through daily activities in life (Streissguth 1999). Gallagher feels that it is extremely important to teach social skills —

> *We taught lots of social skills. We used a fairly structured approach. We practiced often and worked on one skill for two or three weeks. We worked on the skill every day, and we would try and tell everyone in the school what we were working on, even the cafeteria staff. Everyone could provide immediate feedback to that student. We used role-playing and we videotaped. The video-taping was important because these kids don't pick up on things unless they see it four or five times and unless they see their own bodies doing it.*

In order to be successful, students with Fetal Alcohol Syndrome need a great deal of structure and consistency. It is essential that they understand the daily routine and the specific expectations that are required of them. Provision of clear and unambiguous rules that are consistently enforced also is essential (Stratton, Howe and Battaglia 1996). Gallagher found that her students were more successful when they were close to the instruction —

> *Whatever is going on, they have to be close to the source and also have a physical connection to the source of information. They need minimal distraction. They need immediate accurate feedback.*

Important guidelines for teachers include: maintaining a calm and orderly environment; establishing clear and consistent rules; using simple, concrete instructions; helping the student set realistic goals; monitoring performance to facilitate success; balancing structure with responsibility; planning ahead for change; supervising transitions; teaching functional and social skills; and, working closely with the family (Streissguth 1999).

Sometimes the students require relief from the sensory stress they often feel. Gallagher described a strategy she used —

> *We used frequent and fairly isolated breaks*
> *. . . down time. They had a place to sit that*
> *didn't have a lot of stimulation. The breaks*
> *had to be really quiet. We would take one*
> *of the boys out to a quiet part of the hall-*
> *way. This seemed to help him regroup.*

The use of advocates also may be helpful. Advocates could be classroom teachers, teaching aides, social workers, psychologists, or any one who understands the student's unique needs. The advocate would work on the student's behalf and could perform the following tasks: befriending the student; providing a safe haven; talking to the student during times of confusion, misperceptions, perceived injustices; mediating between student and teacher, or between other students; coordinating between school and parents; and giving direct help (Streissguth 1999).

O'Connor pointed to a specific need she would like to see addressed —

I would like to see teachers varying their instruction to accommodate these students. They have to take into consideration the processing problems these students have.

* * * * * * * *

Case History No. 2

Bob was a 15-year-old student with whom O'Connor worked in a vocational school. Many of his behavior problems, she said, were directly related to processing difficulties he had —

> *Bob was in an auto mechanics program. His behaviors included calling out, getting others involved in very off-task behavior . . . sometimes dangerous behavior. He would ignite a lighter around gasoline. He would take parts off a car and hide them. The kinds of things he was doing were attention seeking. He also was avoiding the tasks at hand because he wasn't able to remember what he was supposed to do. For example, if he was given the job to change the oil in a car, he couldn't remember what he was supposed to do. Knowing that he had gone over it several times with the instructor and that he was expected to do it, he would screw around and take parts off of cars or get a group of other kids to misbehave. We focused on eliminating dangerous behav-*

iors first. We left the mischievous behaviors on the back burner. One of the problems was that the instructor was somewhat aggressive. Bob was afraid to go to the instructor for help. I made it clear to the instructor that he needed to remind Bob of what he was supposed to do, even if he had already done that many times before. We made sure that every task he was given he was shown how to do again that day. We kept him to very simple tasks and tried to keep him on the same task. We explained what we were doing, and what he was doing, and why we needed to decrease his dangerous behavior. We made sure he was able to do the task. His behaviors decreased the first week. Within a month he wasn't engaging in any dangerous behavior, just the mischievous behavior. I think he just didn't get what he was supposed to be doing. Once he knew what to do he wouldn't act out.

* * * * * * * *

O'Connor had a genuine affection and empathy for the students with whom she worked who had Fetal Alcohol Syndrome. She spoke of the benefits she received while working with these students —

Probably one of the biggest benefits that you can see right away is, if you are persis-

tent enough, and you continue to follow through with your promises, and you continue to show that you can be trusted, these kids make huge emotional leaps. You can see growth very, very quickly. Although the trust is hard to establish, sometimes it's taken me eight months, once it's there they're very close to you and they do trust very heavily. You can see great emotional strides, and you can also see it in the classroom. Once they're feeling comfortable in the environment you see huge progress.

School curriculums should include lessons that inform students about Fetal Alcohol Syndrome. Since this disorder is preventable, it is vital that students who are vulnerable for substance abuse understand the possible consequences of their actions on themselves and on others.

Fetal Alcohol Syndrome

Fetal Alcohol Syndrome (FAS) is a medical condition characterized by physical and behavioral disabilities resulting from heavy exposure to alcohol before birth. This is a totally preventable disability.

Characteristics:

- Developmental delays (not always)

- Growth deficiency for height and weight

- Abnormal facial features (small space between eyes, flat midface, thin upper lip, pointed ears)

- Motor problems and poor coordination

- Hyperactivity

- Attentional problems

- Learning difficulties

- Processing difficulties

- Emotionally volatile

- Stubbornness

- Defiance

- Immaturity

- Irritability

99

Treatment/Intervention:

- Regular and organized routine
- Provide comprehension modifications
- Role-play and teach social skills
- Set clear limits and follow-through
- Teach multiple-solution generation
- Structure
- Consistency
- Behavior modification
- Metacognition
- External scaffolding
- Communication enhancement
- Self-esteem enhancement

Chapter Six

Anxiety Disorders

Anxiety Disorders fall into the category of overcontrolled behaviors (Epanchin and Paul 1987; Reynolds 1990) that sometimes are difficult to diagnose. Every individual becomes anxious from time to time. When that anxiety becomes immobilizing and interferes with an individual's ability to perform normal tasks related to normal functioning, that individual usually is diagnosed with an Anxiety Disorder. Anxiety Disorders are internalizing disorders because they consist of "relatively covert, often unobservable symptoms" (Reynolds 1990, p. 140). "Anxiety-disordered youngsters rarely pose significant problems to teachers in the classroom, so that teachers may not identify the anxious child as having a significant difficulty worthy of referral (despite an accurate perception of the child as anxious and shy). In fact, teachers often describe anxious children as 'model students' due to their compliance and eagerness to please. Nevertheless, anxiety problems may cause considerable discomfort to the individual child and may impair the youngster's academic and social adjustment" (Strauss 1990, p. 153).

Students who suffer from an Anxiety Disorder frequently show signs of depression, conduct disorder, learning disabilities, and other disorders related to anxiety, such as physical discomfort (Rabian and Silverman 1995). It is important for educators to understand the relationship between these disabilities. "People with persistent fear often feel shame, inadequacy and guilt. They are mercilessly tormented by the fear of fear (i.e., dread of having another panic attack). They may be so easily intimidated that they often become shy and emotionally withdrawn" (Bloomfield 1998, p. 16). These students may develop full-blown Panic Disorder. This disorder is characterized by sudden attacks of terror, usually accompanied by a pounding heart, sweatiness, weakness, faintness, or dizziness. During these attacks, people with panic disorder may flush, or feel chilled; their hands may tingle or feel numb; and they may experience nausea, chest pain, or smothering sensations. Panic attacks usually produce a sense of unreality, a fear of impending doom, or a fear of losing control" (National Institute of Mental Health 2007, p. 2).

According to the United States Surgeon General's 1999 report on Mental Health, about 13 percent of children and adolescents (ages 9 to 17) suffer from Anxiety Disorders. The Surgeon General states that learning disorders and substance abuse disorders in youth may co-exist with anxiety.

There is evidence to suggest that much anxiety is learned, but that biological factors also contribute to the disorder. "Anxiety Disorders of various types tend to run in families, and it is suspected that genetic or other physiological factors may be involved in the origins of these disorders as well as social learning" (Rabian and Silverman 1995, p. 248).

The Surgeon General's report states that "what Anxiety Disorders have in common is a state of increased arousal and fear." There are several theories on the origin of Anxiety Disorders, which include:

> (1) the acute stress response theory that centers on the role of the locus ceruleus in the brain stem;

> (2) anatomical theories that focus on the roles of the hippocampus and the amygdala areas of the brain;

> (3) the complex interaction of chemical "messengers" in the brain, the neurotransmitters;

> (4) psychodynamic theories focused on anxiety symptoms as an expression of underlying conflicts;

> (5) behavioral theories centered on conditioned learning and vicarious learning models;

> (6) cognitive theories involving how people interpret or think about stressful situations.

The Surgeon General's report further goes on to state that "the likelihood of developing an Anxiety Disorder involves a combination of factors. Anxiety Disorders are so heterogeneous that the relative roles of these factors are likely to differ." Factors range from genetics (Panic Disorder) and family history (Obsessive-Compulsive Disorder)

103

to family structure (Separation-Anxiety Disorder) and trauma (Post-Traumatic Stress Disorder).

Self-control training is one of the most commonly used interventions for dealing with children with Anxiety Disorders. In self-control training, fearful individuals learn to talk through a variety of techniques to manage their anxiety. They may learn relaxation, deep breathing, self-reinforcement, self-instruction, visual imagery, or problem-solving strategies (Kauffman 2001).

Dr. William Taylor is an educational counselor who has vast experience working with children and students who have Anxiety Disorders. Taylor described the symptoms —

> *The symptoms are physiological, such as heart pounding, sweating, panic attack clusters, stomachaches, headaches, and fatigue. The child with an Anxiety Disorder often has a general feeling of physical uncomfortableness. There also are behavioral symptoms. These symptoms could include avoidance, reluctance and hesitance.*

One of the biggest obstacles related to individuals who suffer from an Anxiety Disorder is that the individual does not seek assistance. "As long as people consider their anxiety an incorrigible part of their being, they are unlikely to seek diagnosis and treatment. They stay stuck in denial and think, 'That's just the way I am.' The major problem with anxiety, therefore, is under-treatment. Many people postpone treatment hoping the anxiety will simply go away. This may or may not happen" (Bloomfield 1998, p.11).

There are numerous types of Anxiety Disorders. Those that have the most impact on school performance and behavior will be discussed in this chapter, such as, school refusal, separation anxiety, selective mutism, and obsessive-compulsive disorder.

School Refusal

Identification/Causes

School Refusal, also known as school phobia, is one of the more frequent anxiety-based problems of childhood (Epanchin and Paul 1987). Refusal or fear of going to school can be a mild, easily treated disorder, or a serious problem associated with a child who will run away from school the first chance he gets. It should be noted that the student who has school phobia doesn't merely dislike school, but feels like he just cannot be there and often becomes physically sick when forced to attend. "The most common trigger for acute or chronic phobia is either an incident in school, a brief illness, or enrollment in a new school" (Platt 1986, pp. 1- 2).

Characteristics: How School Performance and Behavior Are Affected

School Refusal includes five conditions: "(1) severe difficulty in attending school; (2) severe emotional upset; (3) staying home with the knowledge of parents; (4)

absence of significant antisocial disorders; (5) school absence lasts for several consecutive days, weeks, or even months" (Atkinson, Quarrington and Cyr 1985, p. 84).

The *DSM-IV-TR* links school phobia with Social-Anxiety Disorder. This type of anxiety is characterized as a marked and persistent fear of one or more social situations in which the person is exposed to unfamiliar people or to possible scrutiny by others. The individual fears that he or she will act in a way that will be humiliating or embarrassing. School situations can cause these feelings for many students. Students with a Social-Anxiety Disorder cannot tolerate the fear of humiliation and, consequently, can become school phobic. In children, this anxiety may be displayed by crying, tantrums, fleeing, or shrinking from social situations with unfamiliar people. Additional symptoms include emotional distress in the form of fearfulness, sulking, sore throats, and a general ill-feeling (Platt 1986).

Students who are school phobic usually are identified as truant. "Unlike school truants, for whom they are often mistaken, school phobics will stay home with the parents' knowledge. And unlike the truant, school phobics are often excellent students" (Platt 1986, p.1).

Strategies

Fears associated with school attendance are preventable (King, Hamilton and Murphy 1983). Prevention would involve desensitizing young children to school by introducing future teachers, school routines, or play activities. Transitions to middle school and senior high school also can be made less anxiety-provoking by preparing students for their new environments and new expectations. Making the school environment as non-threatening as possible to the student also will assist him in feeling more comfortable there.

Parents and educators can work together to encourage positive behavior by employing a behavioral approach, "starting gently with the smallest step the child will take in approaching or entering the school" (Platt 1986, p. 2).

"Individual students may need to learn coping skills to deal with irrational thoughts and to learn adaptive behavior (such as asking a teacher or peer for assistance) through modeling, rehearsal, feedback, and reinforcement" (Kauffman 2001, p. 435). Some interventions, based on behavior principles, include (1) desensitization of the child's fear through role-playing or in vivo approximations of attending school for an entire day; (2) reinforcement for attending school even for a minimal amount of time with a gradual lengthening of the time the student would be required to stay in school; (3) matter of fact parental statements that the child will go back to school, avoiding lengthy or emotionally charged discussion; (4) removal of reasons for a child to stay at home (being with a parent, playing games, watching television or other pleasurable activities) (King, Ollendick and Tonge 1995).

Cognitive-Behavior Therapy has been successful in treating individuals with Anxiety Disorders. The cognitive part helps the individual change the thinking patterns that support their fears, and the behavioral part helps people change the way they react to anxiety-provoking situations. "Cognitive–Behavior Therapy can help people with panic disorder learn that their panic attacks are not really heart attacks, and it can help people with social phobia learn how to overcome the belief that others are always watching and judging them. When people are ready to confront their fears, they are shown how to use exposure techniques to desensitize themselves to situations that trigger their anxieties. These students may develop full-blown Panic Disorder. This disorder is characterized by sudden attacks of terror, usually accompanied by a pounding heart, sweatiness, weakness, faintness, or dizziness. During theses attacks, people with panic disorder may flush, or feel chilled; their hands may tingle or feel numb; and they may experience nausea, chest pain, or smothering sensations. Panic attacks usually produce a sense of unreality, a fear of impending doom, or a fear of losing control" (National Institute of Mental Health 2006, p. 8).

Medications to reduce anxiety also may be helpful in certain situations (Campbell and Cueva 1995b). "Systematic desensitization, reciprocal inhibition, and counter conditioning have also been effective in lowering fears of children and adults. The central feature of these procedures involves the individual's gradual and repeated exposure to the fear-provoking stimuli while the person remains unanxious and perhaps engaged in an activity that is incompatible with or inhibits anxiety (such as eating a favorite treat or relaxing comfortably in a chair)" (Kauffman 2001, p. 434).

An important factor in any plan is the inclusion of the student. "The behavioral steps should be developed with the cooperation of the child, if possible. Start with steps of which the child already is capable and build on them. If the child agrees to a step, but is unable to perform it, make the step even smaller, and try again" (Platt 1986, p. 2).

If, as an educator, you believe a student is suffering from an anxiety disorder you should speak with the school social worker or school psychologist. These individuals can suggest to a parent that they talk to the child's pediatrician or family doctor. A physician sometimes can ascertain if the symptoms are related to an anxiety disorder, another medical condition or both. If an anxiety disorder is diagnosed, the student should be brought to a mental health professional who is familiar with anxiety disorders and their treatment.

* * * * * * * *

Case History

Toni Russo is a schoolteacher whose 16-year-old daughter, Holly, became school phobic in 10th-grade. Holly had no difficulty going to school up until this time period, Russo said, and she was an "A" student —

> *Holly had mononucleosis, and she was at home for a couple of weeks. She was sick and then she got well, but when she got well she didn't want to go back to school. She said she didn't feel well. She said she didn't want to go back to school. When she finally agreed to go back she would go, but then she would leave the school without anyone's permission. She just didn't stay and then she just wouldn't go. Sometimes I*

would drive her to school and drop her off in front of the school, and I would go to work. Later, I would find out that she never went into the building. She would walk home. She would tell me that she didn't like school. The teachers weren't friendly and the kids were mean. She said it was very loud and noisy, and school gave her a headache. She said the school made her feel sick, and she had to come home. She was dizzy sometimes. She just didn't want to stay in school. In the beginning, I was sympathetic for several reasons. One, she had just had mono, and she was just get-ting better and she was kind of pale and tired. The second reason was that her father and I were in the process of separat-ing. There was quite a strain on the family. Her father wasn't staying in the house for periods of time. That was difficult for her. After a few weeks, I talked to the school psychologist. He asked if it was possible that she was staying home because she wanted to keep the home intact. That made a lot of sense to me. He also said that the school was not set up to be supportive of sensitive kids. He said it was not a friendly atmosphere. So I was sympathetic on that basis. I spoke to Holly about what the psy-chologist said. She was quiet, but I knew she heard me. However, after another month of school resistance, I was less sympathetic. I finally said to her, "Look there's no reason for you not to go to school. Let's go to school, talk to your guidance counselor and make arrangements so that you can go in the morning from 8:30 until 10:00 and then after a week you can go from 8:30 until 12:00." I wanted her to gradually get back into classes. She agreed to do that, but the first time we tried that, again, she just came home. I got angry and I yelled at her. I really got mad. The following morning I said, "You are a fortunate kid. You're bright, you're physically well, now get the hell to school." I had lost my temper and I felt terrible about it, but it worked. She went to school and stayed until 10:30. She agreed to stay longer and longer. Within two weeks she was going full time to school. She joined the drama club and adjusted.

* * * * * * * *

Separation-Anxiety Disorder

Identification/Causes

Separation-Anxiety Disorder is a disability where a child fears, to the point of panic, the prospect of separation, usually from the primary attachment figure (Epanchin and Paul 1987). When separation-anxiety behavior persists past the age of 4, and causes distress and dysfunction, it is then classified as Separation-Anxiety Disorder (Koplewicz 1989). This disorder affects about 4 percent of all children. While some children outgrow this, others will develop a more extensive form later on as an adult (Frances and First 1998). The *DSM-IV* defines Separation-Anxiety as a developmentally inappropriate and excessive anxiety concerning separation from home or from those to whom the individual is attached.

Individuals with Separation-Anxiety Disorder have had a life-long concern about their health or ability to manage emotional upheavals (Beck and Emery 1985). These individuals have managed to maintain their equilibrium as long as they had available one or more protective figures close by (i.e., parents, siblings, peer group, teacher).

Many professionals feel that Separation-Anxiety Disorder is a major reason why students who have been labeled school phobic don't go to school. Most children experience anxiety about attending school at one time or another, as Taylor previously mentioned —

> *Normal anxiety occurs with just about every child who's going off to school for the first time in kindergarten or to a new school, like a middle school or a high school. With separation anxiety and school phobia, you're going to see panic attacks. The panic attacks are the physiological and the behavioral aspects of the anxiety.*

Separation anxiety is often connected to school phobia. When the attachment between the child and parent is an anxious, dependent attachment, the child is not so much afraid of going to school, but the child is really afraid of leaving Mom. If Mom or Dad was ill or somehow not functioning quite right, it might not be that the child is afraid of school. He might be afraid of leaving Mom. "Is Mom going to be okay or is Dad going to be okay?" One child I worked with had a father with kidney disease. It wasn't really clear in this young child's mind that his father's illness was the basis of his anxiety. It showed up as school phobia. As we got into it in therapy, it became clear that the child was worrying about Dad and Dad's illness.

There are many different family dynamics that can result in school phobia. Personality traits that a child might have also could make that child tend to be more phobic, Taylor said —

Families that tend to move very frequently, where the child doesn't have a chance to develop roots, can cause school phobia. This is because the child doesn't really learn about making relationships or friendships. These kids might have a difficult time in school and might be apprehensive about going to school.

113

Another cause of school phobia, Taylor pointed out, can be related to a social phobia where a child is fearful of a negative evaluation —

> *Kids might be sitting in a classroom petrified that the teacher is going to call on them; they're going to make a mistake; they're going to make a fool of themselves and, while they're sitting there churning all of this, they're creating their anxiety and their panic.*
>
> *With normal anxiety about school, you don't really see any disruption in the attending of school. A child might be anxious about going to school, but this anxiety does not prevent him from going. We do see disruption when there is a disorder. We see apprehension starting the day before. Sunday night is terrible for kids with school phobia . . . days before Christmas vacation ends and school is about to begin again are just awful days for these kids. There's anxious anticipation about going back to school and that often leads to much higher levels of anxiety. There are physiological symptoms that come as a result of that . . . the stomachaches, the headaches, sometimes vomiting. I have had children that I've worked with that have been so afraid that they vomit in the classroom or vomit before school. The child with these types of*

symptoms is not just nervous about school, but actually gets physically sick. What makes school phobia so different from the normal anxiety about going to school is that the student becomes afraid of his own reaction. The way to avoid all this anxiety is to not go to school. The kid wakes up feeling terrible, and he <u>does</u> feel terrible. He complains about the stomachache. The parents are exasperated and not sure what to do. They let the child stay home and 20 minutes later the child is fine.

Characteristics: How School Performance and Behavior Are Affected

Children suffering from Separation-Anxiety Disorder can experience a myriad of emotional and physiological symptoms. Children can encounter an illogical worry that something is going to happen to threaten the integrity of the family and they can become extremely homesick (Koplewicz 1989). Younger children tend to develop gastrointestinal discomfort while adolescents more frequently complain of cardiovascular symptomology (Gittleman-Klein and Klein 1980).

According to the *DSM-IV-TR* individuals are diagnosed with Separation-Anxiety if they experience three or more of the following:

(1) Recurrent excessive distress when separation from home or major attachment figures occurs or is anticipated.

115

(2) Persistent and excessive worry about losing, or about possible harm befalling, major attachment figures.

(3) Persistent and excessive worry that an untoward event will lead to separation from a major attachment figure (e.g., getting lost or being kidnapped).

(4) Persistent reluctance or refusal to go to school or elsewhere because of fear of separation.

(5) Persistently and excessively fearful or reluctant to be alone without major attachment figure, or to sleep away from home.

(6) Persistent reluctance or refusal to go to sleep without being near a major attachment figure, or to sleep away from home.

(7) Repeated nightmares involving the theme of separation.

(8) Repeated complaints of physical symptoms (such as headaches, stomachaches, nausea, or vomiting) when separation from major attachment figures occurs, or is anticipated. The duration of the disturbance is at least four weeks and the onset is before 18 years of age. The disturbance causes significant distress or impairment in social, academic (occupational), or other important areas of functioning.

Strategies

Any treatment approach should include the parents, the school, and the child (Koplewicz 1989). If the child does not respond within a month to a vigorous behavioral child-therapy approach, medication should be added to the treatment regimen. Medications to reduce anxiety may be helpful in certain situations (Gittleman-Klein 1975).

Cognitive-behavioral interventions are employed to modify maladaptive thoughts or beliefs that are theorized to underlie anxiety and other emotional distress (Strauss 1990). Cognitive therapies for children with Separation-Anxiety should be directed toward modifying negative cognitions about one's behavior in the face of a possible threat, and toward building self-esteem. Additionally, other forms of therapy that focus on modifications of negative thoughts about one's competence, like social skills training, could contribute to the efficacy of cognitive therapy in children (Bogels and Ziegerman 2000, p. 310).

A graduated exposure back to school often is recommended. In vivo exposure is a technique designed to slowly reintroduce the student back into the school environment. Students determine the pace and should not be forced to do more than they feel capable of doing. Parents or attachment figures can be available for the students at school. Gradually, the attachment figures are faded out as students gain confidence in the ability to cope with the separation (Scott and Cully 1995).

Backward chaining is another technique that utilizes a graduated exposure to school. With this technique, the student is brought to school by the attachment figure at the end of the day. The student, then, is met by someone and escorted to class. Gradually, the student is taken to school earlier and earlier as he develops coping skills to deal with the separation from the attachment figure (Scott and Cully 1995).

Taylor suggests certain treatment strategies for re-introducing a student back to school —

> *Certainly the effort is to get the child back to school as quickly as possible. But when I say get back to school, I mean just entering the building sometimes. I think steps should be taken as quickly as possible. Not inconsistent with that comment is the other part of the treatment that is with patience. You want to get the child back to school as quickly as possible but it's a patient process. "As quickly as possible" with some kids might be weeks and months. If the anxiety has not been treated by the school or a physician, and it's existed for some months, and panic has really become a pattern, sometimes the family has kind of organized around this problem or disorganized around this problem. Making some changes in this pattern isn't going to happen in a week or so.*

One initial goal in working with children with school phobia is to calm down the situation first, Taylor said —

> *It's an effort to calm down people. They sometimes don't recognize school phobia*

as legitimate. There are many different disorders that kids have these days where educators are kind of "iffy" about whether it's a real thing or not. Part of the task is to inform educators of the validity of the disorder. Then we begin a very gradual desensitization program . . . teaching the parent what the appropriate coaching techniques are. What do you say? What don't you say? I quickly try to get parents to coach their child on how the child can manage his own anxiety rather than have the parent and the child perpetuate the pattern of the child seeking reassurance and the parents giving reassurance. I think that's a problem pattern. My view is that when parents reassure children who are phobic, it really only perpetuates the need for the reassurance. I want to give the parents a different role. I want to give the parents the role of coaching the child on how the child can manage his own anxiety.

An important factor in dealing with students who are school phobic, or who experience separation anxiety, is to give them the tools necessary to help themselves. According to Taylor —

So much of what maintains anxiety for children is fearful anticipation. They get way ahead of themselves. I heard someone say that worry is about the past and the

119

future. Part of what is taught is how to stay in the present. We teach the child how to stay in the present in a very concrete way. I teach them how to create a wall between themselves and their fear. This wall is built by thinking certain ways. The ways to think are this one technique that I call "staying in the present." I teach them how to focus on the here and now in very concrete ways. "I'm sitting at my desk. There's a pad of paper on my desk. My pen is blue. I'm wearing jeans." This is a very simple technique. You can explain it to children of all levels. It's building this wall. While you're thinking "this" you're not thinking "that." A second tool, which is real important to do, is to learn how to accept the fear. I teach the child, "it's only a feeling, it's an uncomfortable feeling but what you need to learn to do is just to leave it alone and it will go away by itself."

When a student experiences separation anxiety or school phobia Taylor suggests —

If a teacher is critical of a child who's anxious, that's just going to plug the fear of negative evaluation right in. The child's going to want to avoid any interaction with the teacher. The teacher needs to acknowledge the anxiety. The thing that is helpful with a child who's anxious is validation and patience. The opposite creates the opposite. I think that an important strategy is to include the child in the thinking about what we're going to do about the problem. I tell parents to do that, too. I would encourage the teacher to sit down and talk to the child. "What would be helpful? How can I help you?" Even that posturing of the teacher is helpful . . . to allow the child to express himself. The teacher can ask, "Would you like to sit up front? Would you like to sit in the back? Would you like to go to the bathroom five minutes after coming into class?" I would say that one guiding principle that a teacher or parents ought to be thinking about when they're having conversations with the child is, how do you take the pressure off the child? What do we need to do that's going to take the pressure off? If a child is really uncomfortable about even entering the building, the behavioral plan has to include how the entry is going to happen. I worked with this one young boy who we negotiated with. Mom drove him to school and they sat in the parking lot and then they went home. After that, he would be okay about simply going up to the building, touching the door, and then going back home. That has to be negotiated with the school. Again, the idea is to think of what steps we need to take the *pressure off. I think there needs to be a plan about using the school nurse in a helpful way. Sometimes children will agree to sit in class with either prescribed breaks to the nurse's office or at least approval that if they have to go to the nurse's office there will be no problem. It should be really clear, however, that if the child is going to sit in the nurse's office it should be for 20 minutes and then back to the class-room.*

Taylor acknowledged that non-medical interventions sometimes just are not enough —

There are some situations where the symp-toms are so extreme that any kind of behav-ioral or cognitive intervention isn't going to work, or perhaps, that intervention is just not enough. Sometimes the situation is too intense and it needs to be controlled medically. Sometimes just an anti-anxiety medication, in really short doses, over a short period of time, is required.

Some suggestions for teachers working with students who have separation anxiety may include: verbally encouraging and praising the student when he is actively involved in the class; giving the student more classroom responsibilities to increase confidence and involvement; not drawing specific attention to the student; and, assist-ing the student by being flexible and by accommodating a re-entry schedule. This will help decrease the student's anxiety (Scott and Cully 1995).

Selective Mutism

Identification/Causes

Although not technically classified as an anxiety disorder, *selective mutism* is often associated with anxiety. "The essential feature of selective mutism is the persistent failure to speak in specific social situations (e.g., school, with playmates, where speaking is expected, despite speaking in other situations). In order to be diagnosed with selective mutism, the person's speech refusal must interfere with educational or occupational achievement or with social communication, and must be going on for at least one month" (The Child Anxiety Network 2001, p. 1).

Research shows that children suffering from selective mutism have had a history of anxiety in social situations from an early age. Many researchers believe that most selective mutism is a form of social phobia. This means that the mutism is caused by an anxiety disorder that reflects inhibited social actions or fear of embarrassment, or concerns that others will judge them negatively. Sometimes family members inadvertently support the child's mutism by speaking for them. Research shows that children suffering from selective mutism, when pushed even mildly to speak for themselves may have overt outbursts and oppositional behavior (NYU Child Study Center 2007).

123

Characteristics: How School Performance and Behavior Are Affected

The school setting frequently offers the greatest challenge for a child with selective mutism. This setting, with many people present and with performance expectations, can heighten the anxiety and, therefore, cause the protective symptom — mutism — to be exacerbated (Schum 2007). Selective mutism can be extremely problematic in the classroom setting. Students will be unable to answer questions or even express needs and ask for assistance when necessary.

Strategies

Currently Behavior Therapy has been the most useful in treating children with selective mutism. Behavior therapy includes the following five steps:

1. anxiety reduction by graduated exposure to feared situations;

2. behavior modification for efforts of graduated exposure;

3. self-modeling of appropriate actions;

4. auditory and video recordings used in settings in which the child is quiet; and

5. cognitive restructuring so that the child externalizes the condition.

"Depending on the extent and duration of the problem, all of these methods may be necessary or an abbreviated use of some techniques may prove useful" (NYU Child Study Center 2007, p. 3).

Medication to treat selective mutism is sometimes used. Its usage is often in conjunction with Behavior Therapy.

It is important for teachers to work with other school professionals, especially speech and language pathologists, psychologists, social workers, family members and those that work with members of the family. "It is also important to implement a nonpunitive, behavioral approach to encourage speech in the classroom and to realize that in many cases successful intervention requires long-term treatment" (Kauffman, 2001, p. 440).

Obsessive-Compulsive Disorder

Identification/Causes

Obsessive-Compulsive Disorder (OCD) is defined as recurrent and distressing thoughts or urges to engage in repetitive and irrational behaviors that create considerable anxiety when resisted (Strauss 1990). There is some evidence that the cause of OCD may be biological since the disorder is more prevalent among relatives of individuals who have this disorder than among the general public (Clarizio 1991).

Characteristics: How School Performance and Behavior Are Affected

According to the *DSM-IV-TR*, obsessions are recurrent and persistent thoughts, impulses, or images that are experienced, at some time during the disturbance, as intrusive and inappropriate and that cause marked anxiety or distress. The thoughts, impulses, or images are not simply excessive worries about real-life problems. The person attempts to ignore or suppress such thoughts, impulses, or images, or to neutralize them with some other thought or action. People recognize that the obsessional thoughts, impulses, or images are a product of their own minds. Obsessions commonly center on aggression (fear of harming others), contamination (concern with germs), sex (homosexuality), exactness, order or symmetry, and scrupulous religiosity (Swedo, Rapoport, Leonard, Lenane and Cheslow 1989). Compulsions are defined by the *DSM-IV-TR* as repetitive behaviors or mental acts that the person feels driven to perform in response to an obsession, or according to rules that must be applied rigidly. The behaviors or mental acts are aimed at preventing or reducing distress, or preventing some dreaded event or situation. These behaviors or mental acts either are not connected in a realistic way with what they are designed to neutralize or prevent, or clearly are excessive. The most common compulsions involve washing, counting, and checking (Clarizio 1991).

Simply put, obsessions are the repetitive thoughts that go on inside the individual's mind, and compulsions are the acts that the individual feels drawn to do. In either case the individual suffering from OCD can be completely immobilized and unable to perform simple actions or tasks. Symptoms can include disruption to daily living activities, effort expended to get through the day, the seemingly senselessness of certain activities, and personal discomfort (Clarizio 1991).

The majority of people with this disorder are secretive. They do not want anyone else to know about their strange thoughts and rituals for fear of ridicule (Clarizio 1991). This fact makes it difficult to identify how many individuals have Obsessive-Compulsive Disorder. "At least some of these students seem to function well during the school day and do not display their rituals in public. Others may use much of their energy and school-day fretting about the rituals (e.g., constantly checking one's fly to see whether the zipper is open) and ruminations (e.g., worrying about whether God will be offended by their sloppy handwriting)" (Clarizio 1991, p. 110).

Also, individuals usually suffer from other symptoms. "Depression is almost always present with individuals with Obsessive-Compulsive Disorder. The long hours spent in repetitive thoughts and actions seem to take the pleasure out of previously enjoyable activities such as sports, reading and sex. Being preoccupied with incessant ruminations and compulsions leaves little time or energy for friends, family, or school" (Clarizio 1991, p. 108).

Although many students will do well in school, others are not so fortunate. "Some students with Obsessive-Compulsive Disorder are perfectionists who want their work to be neat, exact, and precise. Erasures may be commonplace. Falling behind in one's work, slowness despite normal ability, refusing to turn a paper in until it can be checked one more time, difficulty in taking notes (because they try to get every word), and absenteeism (arising from peer ridicule over rituals) also may be symptomatic.

Rough hands that look like eczema may be the result of repeated washing. Friendships may be nonexistent because the ruminations and rituals do not leave much time or energy for friends. Spending from one to three hours a day resisting and/or engaging in obsessions and compulsions is apt to take its toll on scholastic accomplishments and peer relations, and warrants intervention" (Clarizio 1991, p. 110).

* * * * * * * *

Case History No. 1

Judith is a 16-year-old girl with OCD who just completed 10th-grade. She is a bright and friendly girl who has many friends. She attends a small private religious school. There are about 15 students in her class. Judith's mother was concerned about her daughter's behavior —

> *I wanted to bring her to a psychologist over this only she absolutely refused to go. She started crying. She promised that she wouldn't carry it to such extremes and that she would scale it down . . . that she would try and control it. Even with me . . . she gets mad at me if I touch a sponge in the kitchen and then touch food . . . and it's not like my kitchen is dirty. I clean the sponges with bleach every so often, so it's not like it accumulates germs and never gets clean. The things she has to do [ritualistic behaviors] are very time-consuming. She does*

not want to change. She knows she has OCD, but she doesn't feel that it is debilitating.

The frustrations encountered by students with this disorder are evident in the following Question and Answer forum with Judith.

* * * * * * * *

Q. Do you like school?

A. Yeah, it's ok. School is fun because it's a small school, and I'm with all my friends.

Q. Judith, what kinds of rituals do you engage in?

A. I don't touch doorknobs and stuff because . . . the thing is, I don't think it's illogical. Like I don't think it's really ridiculous 'cause I don't think I do things that are so unreasonable. Like I have watched a lot of things on "20/20" [News magazine television program], and they even say that when you open a bathroom door you should use a paper towel cause there are a lot of germs and stuff. So, I usually, if I'm wearing a long-sleeved shirt in the winter . . . I'll use my sleeve to open a door. And I realize that I'm a little more extreme than most people are, but I don't necessarily think it's bad. I mean I like the way it is 'cause I'm comfortable with it.

Q. Do you think about germs a lot? Are you worried about them a lot?

A. Not a lot, but I do think about it. Like at the camp . . . when I was working at the camp, the kitchen . . . no one wore gloves or hairnets, and I wouldn't eat anything that came out of the kitchen and that bothered me. Then I would feel really uncomfortable during lunch. I didn't even like going in there to get more food for the kids. I do wash my hands a lot.

Q. How often do you wash your hands?

A. It depends where I am. Like at the camp, I washed them a lot more. 'Cause every time I would take a kid to the bathroom I would wash my hands, but if I'm at home then I don't have to worry as much so I don't have to wash them as much.

Q. Do you shower more than once a day?

A. Sometimes. It drives my parents crazy.

Q. Did your parents tell you that they don't want you to shower more than once a day?

A. Yeah.

Q. How does your concern about germs affect you in school?

A. It affects me in school not so much. But it does, like I won't touch certain things. Besides doorknobs, in chemistry, I wouldn't wear the goggles cause somebody else had worn them. So I wouldn't always wear them and the teacher would yell at me to put them on. So I put them on really loose so they wouldn't touch me. I was very uncomfortable wearing them. In school I bring my own lunches. If I had to eat school lunches it would be a problem. If there's a table that's dirty I would move.

Q. Do you have trouble eating at other people's houses?

A. Sometimes. It depends where it is. At the camp I never ate anything, and it was hard because I have stomach problems. I'm supposed to eat like every two hours. I get lots of stomachaches. I'm lactose intolerant, and I have a very sensitive stomach. I can't eat anything that's a little old 'cause I'll throw up.

Q. Does anyone give you a hassle about this?

A. My parents used to. They sort of thought it was a little unreasonable. They thought I was washing my hands way too much. They [Judith's hands] used to be really dry, too, and they were cracked.

Q. Did they ever bleed?

A. Yes, they did sometimes. But when you have dry skin . . . that happens to my father even. So it's not like it was just from that, but it definitely added to it and they [parents] would tell me that I shouldn't wash my hands so much.

Q. When they told you that, were you able to stop or do it less, or did you do it secretively?

A. I did it secretively.

Q. Do you ever talk about this to kids in school?

A. Actually, not that I come out and said it, but people notice that I don't touch doorknobs and if they ask me, I'll tell them why. All of these friends know these things 'cause I'm in a small comfortable school, but like when I went to the camp nobody had any idea. My closest friends know.

Q. Do you have any rituals?

A. I definitely have a lot of rituals. I have to do certain things certain ways. Before I do my laundry, first of all, I wash my hands before I touch it, and I take it right out of the dryer and I'll put it away. I won't touch anything else. And if someone else touches it, I'll put it back in the dryer for a little while. And like, before I go to sleep, my bed is like perfectly clean, like my sheets have just come out of the dryer. I haven't touched them with anything else. Before I go into my bed . . . like my pajamas are . . . first of all, I change my pajamas every night and I don't even sit on the couch or anything. After I take my shower, I go straight to bed. In my room everything has to be in a certain place and everything has to be very clean. If someone touches my bed, I'll get really upset and mad.

Q. Do you take a long shower?

A. Yeah. And that used to cause problems sometimes . . . if I use all the hot water or if someone is trying to fall asleep.

Q. Do your rituals and compulsions keep you from doing things that you want to do?

A. There hasn't really been something I wanted to do that I couldn't, but it has been . . . like in camp because I didn't feel comfortable eating the food. It's one of the reasons I stopped working at the camp. When I was a camper I couldn't always eat the food. I brought my own make-your-own-soup things.

Q. Have your parents ever requested that you get help?

A. My parents actually wanted me to for a little while.

Q. If you could change this would you change it?

A. No. It bothers me that some people don't wash their hands after they go to the bathroom.

Q. If there was someone who you really liked, but they weren't that clean, for whatever reason, could you be friends with them?

A. I might feel uncomfortable with them.

Q. I see that you pull your sleeves over your hands. Do you do that often?

A. I always do. It's a habit.

Q. Do you wear sleeves all the times?

A. Yes, but not in the summer.

Q. Are there any other restrictions you feel that you have?

A. Certain restaurants I can't eat in. Like if the floor isn't clean or if there's something on a glass or something then it will be really hard for me to eat anything.

* * * * * * * *

Strategies

Many people do not understand that the behavior
exhibited by individuals with OCD is out of that individual's control. In an effort to help students with this disorder, others may tell them not to worry about whatever it is
they are worried about. They try to reassure the student
that nothing bad will occur if they don't perform compulsive or ritualistic behaviors. Reassurance, however, does
not seem to be effective. "Telling young people that they
are clean, that the door is locked, that their arithmetic
answers are correct does not help" (Rapoport 1989b).
Additionally, family members may get impatient with the
behavior and get angry at the individual. "Helping the
family to understand that Obsessive-Compulsive Disorder
sufferers 'just can't stop' their rituals and that their child
has a serious problem can offer a sense of relief. Opening
communications between parents and the adolescent is
perhaps the first order of business" (Clarizio 1991, p.
113). Friends and family members can play an important
role. Having a supportive relationship can be helpful
(Clarizio 1991).

The most effective psychotherapy treatment for
Obsessive-Compulsive Disorder is exposure and response
prevention (Frances and First 1998). This involves a
repeated and systematic exposure to anxiety, which gradually lessens the need to perform the compulsion and helps
the individual develop a greater sense of self-control.
Behavioral treatment, which recognizes the value of rid-

ding the patient of symptoms, has been successful (Rapoport 1989b). Response prevention is a behavioral treatment whereby the individual is exposed to a situation that triggers the ritual and then is prevented from performing the compulsion or obsession (Wolff and Rapoport 1988).

Other treatments include drug therapy, which has proven to be successful in some cases. Keeping busy and engaging in physical activities or exercise also can alleviate some of the symptoms (Clarizio 1991).

Some students with OCD may not qualify for special school services even though they are emotionally impaired. Although they actually may excel in school, they may be miserable in their private lives. Referral to outside mental health agencies clearly is warranted in these cases, because of the condition's chronic nature and painful consequences (Clarizio 1991).

Mara Davidson has been a therapist for 25 years. She has worked with children and adolescents with OCD. Davidson explained that children with this disorder generally don't see their behavior as problematic —

> *Parents bring in their children. Children don't ask for help . . . not for this. Sometimes you might get a child asking for help later in life . . . maybe 16- or 17-year-olds, particularly with Obsessive-Compulsive Disorder. A younger child . . . often they have no idea that what they're doing is different.*

In many of the cases I work with, there is some family disruption — divorce or separation. That does not necessarily precede the disorder, but it exacerbates the symptoms. Sometimes it [the disorder] comes on as a result of the added stress.

The therapy Davidson employs takes a positive approach. The individual is instructed to examine what works for them and to use this information in a productive manner —

We want people to notice what works for them, even if it seems small. I ask people to notice what works, what makes the situation slightly better. I ask for some detail about that . . . I want them to be specific. I ask them to gather some information about whatever is working, when it's working, or when it used to work. The more information the person can give about that, the more they are able to replicate it and build on it. Everybody involved with that child (the parent, the teacher) is also asked to notice what works. We focus on what works and we ask the person who is doing the behavior to focus on what helps them. People have resources that they are not always aware of. We help people shift from a negative "problem" focus to a more positive "solution-oriented" approach.

* * * * * * * *

Case History No. 2

Davidson worked with an 8-year-old boy who had OCD —

The child had a difficult time doing homework, especially spelling. He couldn't do it without going over it several times and erasing frequently. He couldn't go beyond a certain point. He was having a lot of trouble just completing one word. Learning penmanship was a very difficult task for him, as he would continually think he could never get each letter right. The parents' request was, "We'd like him to be able to do his homework better. Just help him relax more so he can do his homework more easily."

The specifics of the obsession/compulsion were the child would be doing his homework, and he would erase constantly, trying to fix whatever he put down on the paper. He had a problem with schoolwork in the school, but it wasn't as noticeable. At home where he had more time, he could keep doing it. In school there's usually a time limit. There he could mask it a little better by starting the work and not completing it, and think he could finish it at home. The teacher might accept that for a while. So he would do some of the work at school and some at home. I don't know how aware of the problem the teacher was in this particular case.

The primary thing was to have the child experience the anxiety when he would do the task [of the homework], and then teach him tools to deal with it. We helped the child desensitize from the anxiety by teaching him to handle a little at a time, so he would not become overwhelmed by it. Also, the child's mother was helped to understand the tools and how they could help her son. The mother was coached to calm herself and her son, and allow him to become anxious and do the compulsive behavior. We approached it like we were doing an experiment to see if we could help make it easier for him to do his homework.

The object is to teach the child that the anxiety he experiences is okay, it is not a bad thing, that it will not hurt him, that he can learn to tolerate a little at a time —

It is difficult to teach this to the child directly, but the parent can be instructed to help him by proposing to him, perhaps while he is engaged in the homework (and erasing), "How would it be for you if you left that just the way it is and didn't erase it? Take two minutes, I'll set the timer before you erase it and let's see what hap-

pens." During those two minutes the parent is instructed to talk him through, or help him to talk himself through, the anxiety. When he becomes irritable and fidgety we might plan to use a tool like deep breathing or positive self-talk. Children like doing this because it gives them a sense of control, and when they notice that it helps change the way they feel, they are more likely to repeat it.

This child I worked with discovered that crunching paper in his hand helped to relieve some of his anxiety. He took a few shots with the paper into a basket. I suggested to him that when he got stuck on a spelling word he should put it on the bottom of the list so he could go forward to it instead of back to it. His mother was instructed not to allow him to perseverate on his spelling list, but she was to remove the list after a certain amount of time and give it back to him later, and only for a limited time. This gave him a break, which he would not have taken voluntarily. During the break, he was coached to do deep breathing, and he could crunch paper and take shots in the basket if he wanted to. The positive self-talk took the form of how bright he was and how capable he was to do the work, as well as to get through the anxiety. He was taught that anxiety is just a

139

feeling and it passes. He and his mother were also coached to "Stay in the present"; stay focused on the task they were doing at the moment. During four sessions there was some improvement. With his mother's help, he managed to do his homework more successfully for a longer period of time with less erasing and less anxiety.

* * * * * * * *

The Obsessive-Compulsive Foundation recommends several school and classroom accommodations to assist students who suffer from this disorder. Breaking assignments into shorter tasks and modifying expectations based on the individual's needs can be beneficial. Reduction of homework assignments and pre-setting students before activities change also help. Providing extra time for exams and not deducting points for spelling errors sometimes eases a student's need for perfection. Behavior and organization modifications could include setting clear rules and following through on enforcing them consistently, as well as ignoring behaviors that are not seriously disruptive (ocfoundation.org, 2007). All interventions should be based on the individualized needs of the student.

140

Anxiety Disorders

Anxiety Disorders are characterized as over-anxiety, social withdrawal, seclusiveness, shyness, sensitivity, and other indications of retreat from the environment.

Characteristics:

- Self-consciousness
- Hypersensitivity
- Depression
- General fearfulness
- Ritualistic behavior
- Obsessions
- Compulsions

Treatment/Intervention:

- Counseling
- Psychotherapy
- Systematic-desensitization
- Reciprocal inhibition
- Counter-conditioning
- Cognitive behavioral therapy
- Empathy
- Medication

- Deep breathing
- Self-regulatory aids

Chapter Seven

Tourette Syndrome

Imagine you were out in public and you started to shout out inappropriately or make strange faces, or you felt compelled to do other things that were considered inappropriate by others, causing people to stare at you strangely. Now imagine that your body was doing things even though your mind told you not to. For many students with Tourette Syndrome, this is the nightmare they face daily.

Identification/Causes

Tourette Syndrome is a complicated disorder that is difficult to diagnose. It is a neurological disorder that usually has its onset in childhood or early adulthood and is characterized by the presence of both motor and vocal tics. Tics can wax and wane over time, and are exacerbated by physical and emotional stress. "Tics can, at times, be suppressed voluntarily. An urge to engage in the tic behavior often precedes the action and attempts to suppress the tic often are accompanied by an increase in this sensation. The performance of the tic can be accompanied by a sense of relief" (Steingard and Dillon-Stout 1992, p. 849).

The cause of Tourette Syndrome is not completely understood, although there appears to be a clear genetic disposition. "Apart from the inherited genetic vulnerability to Tourette Syndrome, it also has been suggested that perinatal insults (e.g., birth injuries) and more recently (and somewhat speculatively) infections with streptococci or viruses may affect the expression of Tourette syndrome" (Robertson, 2000, p. 2).

Although scientists do not understand exactly what causes Tourette Syndrome, they have a fairly clear understanding of what causes the tics that go along with the condition. "Presently researchers believe that tics are caused, at least in part, by nerve cells in the brain that are sensitive to the brain chemicals dopamine and/or serotonin. These two chemicals are neurotransmitters, meaning they ordinarily help transmit signals from one nerve cell in the brain to the next. Dopamine is a key brain chemical in the parts of the brain that control movement, and serotonin is another brain chemical that regulates a number of brain activities including pain, emotions, and movement. Tics are involuntary and reflect the misfiring of nerve cells involved with movement" (Hansen 2007, p. 5).

Not all children who have tics have Tourette Syndrome. "The essential features of Tourette Syndrome are the presence of multiple motor tics (twitches) and one or more vocal tics (or noises). The tics may appear simultaneously or at different times throughout the illness. Typically, the tics occur many times a day, in bouts, and must have been present for at least one year if a diagnosis is to be made" (Baron-Cohen 2001, p. 45).

There is no typical student with Tourette Syndrome. "The range of Tourette Syndrome behaviors displayed by children is wide. These vary amongst individuals and sometimes from day to day for individuals. One tic may be recurrent, for example, eye blinking, head jerking or shoulder shrugging. Others might appear and disappear unpredictably" (Wilson and Shrimpton 2003, p. 2).

Difficulties in the identification of this disorder arise because symptoms seem to come and go. Observers, including parents and teachers, often conclude that the child actually has control over his or her actions and may be indulging in these manifestations deliberately. "Even where the manifestations are mild they are likely to be interpreted as an indication of a deeper psychological problem or as an odd mannerism, rather than what it is defined as in Tourette's: a specific symptom of neurological disorder" (Teitelbaum 1979, p. 89).

Characteristics: How School Performance and Behavior Are Affected

Individuals with Tourette Syndrome suffer from a plethora of symptoms that cover a broad range, from very mild to quite severe, and usually are worse during adolescence. Although Tourette Syndrome lasts throughout one's life, some people experience a complete remission or a marked improvement in their late teens or early 20s. Only about 10 percent of the children who inherit the gene will have symptoms severe enough to require medical attention (Colligan 1989).

Contrary to public belief, only 30 percent of individuals who have Tourette display coprolalia (the uncontrolled uttering of obscenities), according to the Tourette Syndrome Association. Coprolalia can be such a shocking symptom that the entertainment industry often dramatizes it, thus, the public is familiar with this characteristic. Other specific tic symptoms of Tourette Syndrome can include: involuntary body movements; uncontrollable vocalizations and/or verbalization; echolalia (repeating the words of others); palilalia (repeating one's own words); and compulsive or ritualistic, repetitive behavior.

In addition to tic symptoms, many children with Tourette have associated disorders. Attention Deficit Hyperactivity Disorder and Obsessive-Compulsive Behavior often accompany tic symptoms. Additionally, many individuals with Tourette Syndrome also suffer from anxiety and depression (Robertson 2000).

Numerous behavior problems may be associated with the syndrome. At least 50 percent of children with Tourette Syndrome satisfy the diagnostic criteria for Attention Deficit Disorder (Colligan 1989). ADD and hyperactivity may precede the onset of tics and may worsen tic severity. The stress of trying to remain quiet, and the stress of trying to keep their bodies still may exacerbate the increasing difficulty students have with attention. Accompanying the various behavior disorders associated with Tourette, the child also may have emotional problems that simply may co-exist with the disorder, or are, perhaps, secondary to it.

Obsessive-compulsive symptoms frequently occur in patients with Tourette Syndrome (Steingard and Dillon-

Stout 1992). "In Tourette Syndrome, the obsessions often involve thinking about violent scenes, sexual thoughts, and counting (arithmomania), and the compulsions have to do with symmetry, 'evening up,' lining things up and getting things 'just right'" (Baron-Cohen 2001, p. 47).

Students with Tourette, in combination with associated disorders, have tremendous difficulty in school. Bouts of episodic rage sometimes are a feature of the syndrome. This is particularly true for children who also have ADHD. Students who have explosive outbursts of temper and aggressive behavior are the most difficult to manage. "Such children are best viewed as having a thin barrier between aggressive thoughts and aggressive acts. In other words, it is simply easier for them to lose control of their temper and harder to restrain themselves. Thus, while they deserve patience and understanding, they still must be held responsible for their behavior" (Bruun and Bruun 1994, p. 119).

Other symptoms of Tourette can include aggressive, antisocial, self-injurious, and inappropriate sexual behaviors (Bruun and Bruun 1994). Depression, phobias, anxiety, and sleep disorders also are characteristics.

Students with this disorder may have specific learning disabilities, due to tics, obsessive-compulsive behavior or attention deficit hyperactivity disorder, or the side effects of medication. "Learning disabilities related to reading, handwriting, spelling and math are very common. These problems are present in 23 percent, nearly one out of four, children with Tourette Syndrome" (Burd 2007, p. 208).

147

"Children with Tourette Syndrome may also have problems with attention and impulsiveness, even if they do not have the full Attention Deficit Hyperactivity diagnosis" (Baron-Cohen 2001, p. 47).

Other educational issues may arise that may not be so obvious. "Tics may interfere with the flow of a child's writing, reading, speech, attention . . . or really, any learning activity" (Kerbeshian 2007, p. 65).

These children usually can have severe emotional difficulty dealing with the disturbing behavior they are unable to stop. "Children with Tourette Syndrome are often aware of the impulses that precede tics or other problem behaviors. Though they may struggle to gain control, they inevitably lose the battle. Feelings of helplessness, shame, and guilt are engendered by this failure and must be dealt with" (Bruun and Bruun 1994, p. 120).

There have been numerous studies documenting that stress has been shown to increase the severity of tics (Robertson 2000).

Monica Williams is a special education teacher who has worked with approximately 20 students, 14- and 15-years old, who have Tourette Syndrome. She has worked in three private schools designed for students with special needs and currently works as a consultant teacher in a vocational program. According to Williams —

> *Having a student with Tourette Syndrome can be a major disruption. You need to be constantly focusing on what that student is doing. All the students I worked with who had Tourette had difficulty managing themselves. It was as if these students were*

*always bottled-up. Many of the kids had
Attention Deficit Hyperactivity Disorder
also. These students were always trying to
hold something in that they couldn't. It was
like an inner battle for them. There was a
lot of impulsivity. When there is a part of
your body that you can't control it affects
your whole life. You can't concentrate.
Their school work definitely suffered.*

According to Williams, specific situations for some
can cause more difficulties than for others —

*The lunch room was a nightmare for these
students. There was too much stimulation
. . . the other kids . . . so much noise . . . so
much walking around. One student begged
me to let him eat lunch in the room. I had
another student who wouldn't sit at the big
lunch table. He sat at a small little round
table. He went there on his own with
another student.*

Many children with this disorder are alienated by
peers who have difficulty understanding the unusual and
sometimes outrageous behavior caused by this syndrome.
"In our imperfect world, parents of other children discour-
age such social relationships with Tourette sufferers and
thus make them bear a double burden: a neurological
impairment, plus a social deprivation" (Teitelbaum 1979,
p. 90).

Middle school and high school can be particularly
problematic. Social situations can be complicated and

painful for even the typical student. Adding the symptoms of Tourette syndrome to the situation can immensely magnify problems (The Tic.info 2007).

Students are forced to deal with feelings of frustration caused by an inability to control their actions and by feelings of alienation. They developed a built-up anger and rage. Williams observed this with some of her students —

> *These students get out-casted. They would get taunted by the other students. The students with Tourette Syndrome had a very hard time making friends. Even if they weren't ostracized by other students in their class, other students would tease them in the hall. The kids with Tourette would fight. There was one student of mine who ended up in time-out because he was trying to fight this other student who was picking on him. This student [the student with Tourette Syndrome] had so much anger in him. Finally, I told him that I was going to leave him alone for a minute. When I came back he was balled up and crying. He was crying hysterically. It just all came out for him. The anger that these students feel comes from having to constantly prove themselves. They have to prove that they're cool and tough and not any different from anyone else. These students can be the nicest kids in the world and, in a way, they are so normal because*

they just want to fit in. Because they are always feeling targeted, they try to compensate for their disability and then you get behavior problems. Many of these kids have been picked on their whole life, and they are very sensitive about things, no matter how tough they act, they are very sensitive.

Strategies

The difficulty for many educators is determining when behavior is in the control of the student and when it is not. "Distinguishing between involuntary and voluntary behaviors becomes even more complicated when a behavior that may be partly beyond control also is socially unacceptable. For example, even though a child with Tourette Syndrome may have a severe spitting tic and poor impulse control, he must learn to control the impulse to spit in other people's faces" (Bruun and Bruun 1994, p. 119).

Often students with Tourette Syndrome try to suppress their tics. "Tic suppression requires much energy and can cause stress which may interfere with a student's ability to concentrate on classroom tasks" (Wilson and Shrimpton 2003, p. 5). It is not a good idea for educators to encourage or tell students with Tourette Syndrome to suppress tics. Unfortunately many typical students and adults have a negative response to students with Tourette Syndrome, which in turn increases tics and generates self-doubt. "However, regardless of teacher acceptance of tics students still may try to suppress tics regardless because of the concern for unwanted reactions of peers and others" (Wilson and Shrimpton 2003, p. 4).

In order to be successful in school, a student must have an empathetic teacher. "The teacher must make a special effort to deal with situations in a way which not only does not damage the child's self-esteem, but which also communicates to the child that he or she wants to help and understands that the Tourette student cannot help some of the behavior which is disturbing the class. If the child feels that the teacher is a 'friend,' some progress is practically assured" (Teitelbaum 1979, p. 90).

One strategy currently being used to deal with tics is called Habit Reversal Training. The idea behind Habit Reversal Training is "replacing a tic with a more socially acceptable behavior. For example, a person with an arm-jerking tic might run his fingers through his hair at the end to make the tic look like a more purposeful behavior. However, the ultimate goal of Habit Reversal Therapy is not simply to camouflage or hide the tics, but, rather, to greatly lessen, and in some cases, eliminate the premonitory urge and/or the tic altogether" (Piacentini 2007, p. 98).

Since the symptoms of Tourette Syndrome can be bizarre and disturbing to other students in the classroom and school, it is vital that these students are educated about it. The skilled and sensitive teacher who can enlist the aid and understanding of peers is of inestimable help to the student with the syndrome (Teitelbaum 1979). Williams also stressed how essential it was to educate the other students in her class about Tourette, and that it not only benefited the student who had Tourette Syndrome,

but also other students who had specific problems or disabilities —

> *Educating the other students was very*
> *important. One year I got a student with*
> *Tourette Syndrome in the middle of the*
> *year. Before this student even arrived I*
> *talked to the other students about this par-*
> *ticular disorder. I had them read a really*
> *good article about Tourette. The students*
> *became very interested in it and then they*
> *started talking about their own problems.*
> *We always encouraged that in my class-*
> *room. One student had Traumatic Brain*
> *Injury and he spoke about it, and then*
> *another student talked about being manic-*
> *depressive. Kids can be pretty understand-*
> *ing. I find the more you talk about things*
> *the better off everyone is.*

It can be daunting for an educator to work with a student with Tourette Syndrome. "The knowledge and skills
required of teachers working with students with other
chronic medical problems and learning disabilities also
apply to helping children with Tourette Syndrome" (Wilson and Shrimpton 2003, p. 14).

Before a behavior plan is developed, educators
should have a complete understanding of the particular
student. "Treatment entails comprehensive holistic care of
the patient, who, in addition to tics, may have a myriad of
other disabilities associated with Tourette. Careful evaluation for the presence of associated problems is important

before a treatment plan is made. Treatment may necessitate medication, supportive psychotherapy, behavior therapy, family or marital therapy, and changes in the school program" (Bruun and Bruun 1994, p. 118). Educators also need to be aware of the possible side effects of medications used to treat tics and related disorders. Medications can cause symptoms of depression, apathy, restlessness, anxiety, tension, and irritability, as well as school phobia and sleep problems (Bruun and Bruun 1994).

A reduction of stress and anxiety often improves behavior and tic symptoms in students with Tourette Syndrome. For these students, instruction in relaxation and body control is an important activity (Teitelbaum 1979).

When a student with Tourette is having a bout of tics, as little attention as possible should be drawn to that student. A private place of refuge for the student is recommended so that he can avoid social embarrassment. Although tics can be suppressed for periods of time this may result in an increase of rebound tics. "Teacher and child should work out an acceptable system so that the child may leave the room when he or she feels an eruption coming on" (Teitelbaum 1979, p. 91).

Providing metacognitive training to help a student monitor his or her behavior can be quite helpful. The benefits can be seen in school as well as in the daily life of that student. "When employing behavioral treatments for Tourette Syndrome, self-monitoring should be recommended as the initial behavioral approach" (Peterson and Azrin 1992, p. 173). (Metacognition is discussed in Chapter Eleven.)

A carefully designed behavior modification plan can be useful. Target behavior for change, however, should not include behavior over which the student has no control. An immediate time-out period for bad behavior or a small daily reward for good behavior can be effective. Compulsive and ritualistic behaviors should be tolerated to a point, but they must be stopped when they become excessive or disturbing to other children (Bruun and Bruun 1994). (Behavior Modification is discussed in Chapter Eleven.) Williams felt that some of her students had some success using a behavior modification program —

> *We had a point system within the classroom. They had a point sheet for every single period. We had to really break it down for them. The kids seemed to respond well to this because they saw immediate rewards.*

Since students with this disorder may have difficulty completing assignments and getting tasks done, it is essential that a well thought-out plan of action be incorporated to help these students with their individual academic difficulties. Williams suggested —

> *For one of my students who just couldn't get things done I had an index card on his desk with a list of things he could do when he was done doing his work. I broke things down into every single step so that I wouldn't have to keep telling him what to do. When he wasn't being productive that*

155

was when the problems would start. His productivity really increased. It really helped. I found that he liked to cross off things from his list. He felt that he had accomplished things. When he finished something on his list he could then choose what he wanted to do next. Choices seem to really work well with these students. We tried to do hands-on activities and give them a chance to move around as much as possible. Sitting at their desks is hard for them. One of my students was the mail carrier in-between the buildings. He did the inter-office mail.

Suzanne Jefferson is the president of a local chapter of the Tourette Syndrome Association. She also is a certified teacher and the parent of a 10-year-old daughter who has Tourette. Jefferson said —

The range [of Tourette Syndrome symptoms] is tremendous. It can be extremely mild, a few tics here and there, a couple of eye blinks, a headshake and a snort here and there, and you go on with your day and it's really not a problem. It can be severe. Everything you do is impacted . . . absolutely everything you do . . . from putting on your clothes, to going to the bathroom, to trying to write your name. Some folks have full body thrusts. Some have it primarily in one area or another. Most have it in their head, neck shoulders, or arms, but feet and legs can be involved and in something internal where you can't see what is going on. A lot of times there are things you can't see. And a lot of times there are mental tics, which are kind of like obsessions where they get kind of stuck on something . . . whether it's something they just heard or something they thought of or something along those lines, keeps repeating in their head. And you can't see that either, so you don't know why this kid is having a problem. Something is going on in their [mind] preventing anything else from coming in.

The child's behavior is impacted in a big way, Jefferson said, because the kids are stigmatized —

They're not understood. For some kids, though, they do pretty well. They can use it as an advantage. They can make it look like something it's not and laugh it off. They can use a sense of humor if they have one and it helps them. Some make a couple of good friends and just stick with them and go along. Some have a lot of trouble. They're ostracized, and not even so much just ostracized, but actually attacked. They're not just ignored, they're out there being picked on. That's difficult. Then you've got kids getting into physical fights.

157

In one case I know of a kid being hospitalized because he couldn't stop saying the word "nigger." When he was confronted by several kids about it at the same time, the stress level went up, it just came out more and it was seen to be rude and abusive on his part. They just beat him senseless.

There are ways teachers can help, Jefferson said —

I think they need to be prepared ahead, and they need to evaluate whether or not they can handle it. If they can't, they need to be big enough to say, "I need to be reassigned this year." A bad match between teacher and student is not going to work under any circumstance. It's going to be really bad for the kid. The kid will lose at least a year and that's not fair to him. Teachers who are flexible and tolerant, and nurturing, and have a good sense of humor, naturally, are probably the best ones to work with these kids. Teachers who must have total control of their room . . . who must be in charge always, should not take these children. You want structure, but it has to be flexibly administered. If they have no structure, they're lost. They need to know, generally, "this is our schedule." You go from A to B to C to D. Do they have to have the exact time? I don't think so. If you make it too rigid you run the risk of kicking in the

OCD [Obsessive-Compulsive Disorder] or the anxiety, if the schedule isn't perfect on some day. For my daughter, in fact, I sometimes have to pre-set her for chaos because I don't know what we're stepping into. If we're going somewhere where I've never been and she's never been, I usually go, "well, this is how this is gonna go. We'll do A, B, C and this is what you can expect." And she gets ready to go and we do it. But sometimes I don't know. I haven't been to a new place either. So I set her up for, it could be this or it could be that. We might have to listen; we might have to wait. It might be completely different from anything we've ever done. It might be chaos, and she goes, "okay." And then she's ready for anything. If they know what to expect and what's expected of them, you have the best chance of having a successful experience.

As far as having social or behavioral issues in the classroom, Jefferson said —

Well, that's a tricky one. For these kids there's so much that goes into what's causing their problems. Whoever the adult is in that situation, whether it's the teacher or an aide, a special ed. teacher, an O.T. . . . that person has to identify what's causing the problem . . . what's the trigger and

159

what's happening to the kid. If the child is verbal enough to tell you, "this is hard for me right now because . . . " then you can work out a solution fairly easily. If the child isn't really that aware or that verbal to tell you, then it's tougher. You need to notice what the environs are that might trigger those things. You also need to know the nature of their obsessive-compulsive things . . . what they're obsessing on right now . . . and what was an obsession several months ago might not be anymore. A one-to-one thing for a while I think is good. Get one kid with the other one . . . a buddy . . . probably someone who's not very outgoing. You want them to be able to interact comfortably. Sometimes a shy person . . . the one with the disability will be able to understand that so much better than a non-disabled peer and will just kind of draw them out naturally. Sometimes a person with a similar disorder who's higher functioning will draw them out because they can work together and they naturally understand one another. I would want to see that the child with Tourette Syndrome is included in some social activities within a smaller group within the classroom. The group work should occur and change . . . not everyday. You want to have the same group for awhile till they establish some rapport and then you might want to add someone in and change someone out so they get to know everyone in a comfortable way.

Other specific interventions that are helpful, according to Jefferson —

Behavior modification can be helpful if you are addressing the right thing. If you're trying to address the symptoms of the disorder, you're going to cause all kinds of havoc. It can be helpful in training routines and it can be helpful in delaying gratification or impulsivity, or some of the ADHD [Attention Deficit Hyperactivity Disorder] things. I think it's really important to help children learn to be self-aware. That's the critical thing because these kids that are not self-aware . . . if they even know their tics and things are going on, they don't necessarily know how it's impacting the kids around them. I know with my daughter it took a very, very long time and a lot of work in helping her understand what her body was telling her . . . what that means . . . what feelings that's part of . . . what you can do to relieve that. They need that self-awareness. They need to know what the body is telling them. They need to start identifying that something's going to happen soon. They need to develop a set of

161

skills. "What can I do because these are things that are going to happen? What am I going to do to divert it?" The teacher has to be always aware of this child . . . always monitoring. Initially the teacher and the parent kind of have to be the child's self-monitor. You might talk to the child, "it looks like you're feeling edgy." You don't want to tell them, "hey, you're edgy go do this," but you might say, "It looks like you're uncomfortable right now. What's wrong? Is there anything I can do?" After a while they start to learn it for themselves. Then they can say, "I'm edgy, but I don't know what to do about it. I feel like I'm going to throw this off the table." That's where you want to get them so they can tell you this before they do it. For a while you have to tell them what to do. If they have no ideas . . . first you want to see if they have any ideas. If they don't have any ideas, then you're going to have to give them ideas. Then after a while they're going to learn to develop their own ideas and basi-cally what you want to train over the long haul is a self-monitoring, self-regulating system. That's what they're going to need when they're out of school.

It may be necessary to modify the classroom environ-ment, Jefferson explained —

*I would only have out and visible what
you're working on at the time. Everything
else would be behind a closed door of some
kind. Never have stuff out that the child
isn't actually using. Make sure there's no
extra distraction. I'd have a comfortable
area with a carpet and beanbags . . . a
place where the student can just go and
relax whenever he needs to . . . a time to
read a book or be with some toy or whatever makes him comfortable. That would
be in the classroom as part of the classroom, not as a separation thing. I would
also have a more structured space outside
of the classroom when that's just not going
to be enough — a place that has limited
stimulation but has comfortable stimulation.*

Most importantly, Jefferson summarized —

*The overall approach with kids with
Tourette and co-morbid disorders would be
to look at the total picture of the child. Your
ultimate goal is, again, the self-awareness
training . . . what to do about that and having them do it themselves. That's your ultimate goal . . . To get there I think you're
going to need to provide the student with
social and occupational help. With children with Tourette Syndrome they have the
skills, but because of the symptoms they*

can't access them. You need the staff to have a lot of preventative strategies on hand. Any known triggers, you avoid them. You work around them. If you know what the obsessions are then you don't hang a picture of the obsession in the classroom. The pre-sets are critical. If you can keep that child informed of everything that's happening and everything that's usual that's going to happen . . . things like that are very helpful. Allow the child to make a lot of the choices. I always give two. If I give more it gets to be too much. If I give only one than I'm setting up for a power struggle.

* * * * * * * *

Case History

Tyler Sommers is an 8-year-old boy who has Tourette Syndrome. He also has two associated disorders, Attention Deficit Hyperactivity Disorder and Obsessive-Compulsive Behavior. Currently he is in the third-grade and in a regular education class with the support of a one-to-one aide and a consultant special education teacher. Tyler is a bright and articulate boy who speaks with a prolonged stutter. In addition to previously mentioned symptoms, Tyler has hand tremors and sometimes body tremors. He used to experience facial and vocal tics that included eye-blinking, grimacing, barking, clearing his throat and clucking. Since taking clonodine, he no longer experiences these tics. Last year, he had great behavioral difficulties in second-grade that included verbal and physical opposition. By February, he was removed from his class and spent the majority of the day in a one-on-one situation, and did much better, as his mother attested —

Last year, he was having outbursts in the classroom. He was frustrated. The way I perceived it, he would become overwhelmed and he would act out. He would verbally challenge and refuse to do things and then would act out. The staff would then jump into a restraint. He has sensory issues so this would usually make things worse. I felt his teacher lacked an open mind. The minute Tyler did something wrong, in her eyes, she went on the warpath. She was working to get him out. I felt that she had a bias against him from day one.

The third-grade teacher's attitude is so great. She is accepting of Tyler and is willing to do what she needs to in order to accommodate him in the classroom. They have an outlet for him, another room where, if he needs to, he can go. The special education teacher this year is amazing. She has a great background and has experience working with students who have Tourette Syndrome. Tyler's aide is wonderful. She pre-sets Tyler. She is so in tune with him. She knows when he needs a break, before he does. She gives him space. When he asks to go to special area classes alone she lets him do it. This gives him confidence.

I think teachers have to be diligent in learning about Tourette Syndrome. Sometimes when it looks like a student is engaged in a power play it may be that it's part of the syndrome. And believe me, as a parent, I don't always know, and I know it's hard. I wish teachers would defer to the characteristics of the disability before they punish or say something that is going to hurt the child. These children often can't help it and can't control their bodies.

We never excuse bad behavior. He knows that he is held accountable, and that includes in school. I try to be fair in disciplining him.

I have never heard him express, "I feel so sorry for myself. Why did this happen to me?" Tyler has so much empathy. I don't know if this is because he has a disability or because of just who he is . . . he is so compassionate and so sensitive and caring about other people.

Tyler's progress in the regular third-grade program has greatly improved, as evidenced in the following Question and Answer forum with him.

* * * * * * * *

Q. How is school going for you this year?

A. Very good.

Q. So you like school?

A. Yes.

Q. Tell me what you like about school.

A. I like my teacher, my classmates, and the things we do in class.

Q. Can you tell me some reasons why you like your teacher?

A. Because she's nice. She's fair and she's strict.

Q. Is there anything you don't like about school?

A. No. I like mostly everything about school.

Q. Is there anything in school that makes you mad?

A. Sometimes when people do or say means things to me.

Q. Does that happen a lot?

A. No.

Q. Who says mean things to you?

A. Kids.

Q. When you are having a difficult time how do the teachers help you?

A. They explain things to me and they might explain what they say . . . what it means.

Q. Last year was a harder year for you wasn't it?

A. Yes, because I didn't really have the right medicine to help me control myself like I do now.

Q. What does it mean to you to have Tourette Syndrome?

A. It means that I can't quite control my body as well as other people.

Q. What would you like me to tell teachers about working with kids who have Tourette Syndrome?

A. Well, I know one thing. I can't keep my hands still. When I draw sometimes it doesn't come out as good as a normal kid's drawing.

Q. Do you want teachers to understand that there are times when things are going to be harder for you than other kids?

A. Yes.

Q. Is there anything about school that you would like to change?

A. I guess there isn't anything.

Q. Would you say the same was true last year?

A. No!

Q. What would you have changed last year?

A. I would have taken medicine so that I could have been back in the classroom.

Q. Were you much happier in the classroom?

A. Yes.

Tyler seemed to feel that his behavioral problems in second-grade had to do entirely with himself. As is common with students who take medications for issues related to behavior, they feel it is the medication that helps them behave and not their own efforts.

Tourette Syndrome

Tourette Syndrome is an inherited neurological, multiple tic disorder.

Characteristics (may include):

- Involuntary body movements
- Uncontrollable vocalizations and/or verbalization
- Coprolalia (uncontrolled uttering of obscenities)
- Echolalia (repeating the words of others)
- Palilalla (repeating one's own words)
- Compulsive or ritualistic behavior; repetitive behavior
- Associated Disorders:
  - Learning Disabilities
  - Attention Deficit Hyperactivity Disorder
  - Obsessive-Compulsive Behavior
  - Difficulty with anger

Treatment/Intervention:

- Medication (not always successful)
- Educating class members about Tourette
- A moderately structured classroom
- Opportunities for physical movement

- External scaffolding
- Refuge when symptoms become intensified
- Metacognition
- Stress relief
- Assistance with social isolation
- Teaching cause and effect
- Teaching responsibility for choice
- Teaching anger management
- Teaching alternative behavior (substitute)
- Pre-setting

171

Chapter Eight

Asperger Syndrome

Some of the most interesting students to work with are students who have Asperger Syndrome. The unique characteristics these students have make their behavior fascinating. Asperger Syndrome is "quintessentially a disorder of human relationships." These individuals, however, can have characteristics that are charming (Tantam 1987).

Identification/Causes

Asperger Syndrome falls within the category of Pervasive Developmental Disorder (PDD), which is described in the *DSM-IV-TR* (2000) as a severe and pervasive impairment in the development of reciprocal social interaction or verbal and nonverbal communication skills, or when stereotyped behavior, interests, and activities are present. "Asperger Syndrome is conceptualized as a disorder characterized by autistic social dysfunction, idiosyncratic interests, normal intelligence and normal language development" (Ghaziuddin and Butler 1998, p. 43). There is some debate about whether it is a disorder unto itself or a form of high-functioning autism (Cohen 1998). Autism is a neuro-developmental disorder characterized by a distinct pattern of social deficits, communication impairment and a restricted range of interest (Lord and Rutter 1995).

Symptoms and difficulties caused by Asperger syndrome are evidenced from birth or soon after, and continue throughout life, although some people learn to cope better as they get older. Asperger Syndrome affects approximately one student per 250 students and males are diagnosed more often than females. The average age of diagnosis is around 9 years old, but it is entirely possible for an individual to remain undiagnosed well into adulthood (Powell 2004).

There is no medical test for Asperger Syndrome at this time. Diagnosis usually is based on parental interviews, observations, and interactions with the child. Often requests for teachers and parents to fill out behavior questionnaires are used for diagnosing Asperger Syndrome (Hansen 2007).

Characteristics: How School Performance and Behavior Are Affected

Individuals with Asperger Syndrome seem to strike others as being strange and awkward. They "often appear eccentric or emotionally disturbed. In spite of good academic performance, these children seem to lack common sense" (Cohen 1998, p.12). "They may learn many facts about the world, but their knowledge seems to remain curiously fragmented. They somehow fail to put their experience and knowledge together to derive useful meaning from these often unconnected bits of information" (Frith 1997, p. 4). Students with this disorder have difficulty generalizing information. They frequently have problems applying information and skills across settings and with different people. Additionally, they have problems integrating learned knowledge and experience (Myles and Southwick 1999).

There seems to be a broad range for how individuals with Asperger Syndrome do in school and in society at large. "Some show extreme behavior difficulties, others are gentle and easy to manage. Some suffer from specific learning disabilities and do badly at school. Others do very well academically and have university degrees. Some may find a niche in society and lead a reasonably contented life, but others become outcasts and remain misfits" (Frith 1997, p. 5).

One of two key hallmarks of this disorder is an impairment in social interaction due, in part, to communication difficulties. These students appear socially inept in their approaches and interactions (Frith 1997). Much of this has to do with a seeming inability to read verbal and non-verbal communication. They fail to develop peer relationships appropriate for their age group. "They seldom enter the natural flow of small-talk, and their use of language and gesture is often stilted. Even those individuals who are very able intellectually and have coped well with their handicap will strike one as strange. This strangeness may be perceived as anything from chilling cold-bloodedness to endearingly old-fashioned pedantry" (Frith 1997, p. 5). Some specific interactional characteristics include impairments in reciprocal social interactions (inability and/or lack of desire to interact with peers, lack of appreciation of social cues, and socially and emotionally inappropriate behavior) (Gillberg 1997, p. 122). Speech and language problems may include delayed development, superficially perfect expressive language, formal language, peculiar voice characteristics, and comprehension impairments that include misinterpretation of literal or implied meanings. Non-verbal communication problems may include limited use of gestures, clumsy body language, limited or inappropriate facial expression and stiff gaze (Klin and Volmar 1995). Students with Asperger Syndrome may have extensive vocabularies, but their speech is usually atypical. "They may quote a favorite movie or TV show whenever asked questions. They may talk like 'little professors,' lecturing with words and phrases far more grown up than those used by peers. They may have trouble modulating their tone of voice — always too loud or too soft. Or they may speak with exaggerated emotion — or no emotion at all" (Hansen 2007, p. 12).

Some individuals with Asperger Syndrome have difficulty understanding the emotions and mental states of people in social situations. Eight problems associated with this difficulty include: difficulty explaining one's behavior; difficulty understanding emotions; difficulty predicting the behavior or emotional states of others; problems understanding the perspectives of others; problems inferring the intentions of others; lack of understanding that behavior impacts how others think or feel; problems with joint attention and other social conventions; and problems differentiating fiction from fact (Myles and Southwick 1999).

Poor awareness of others leads to other behavioral problems such as contradicting or being noncompliant toward teachers, not sharing or allowing other children to join in his or her games, making inappropriate comments in class, talking too loudly, and over-reacting to losing (Powell 2004).

The second hallmark of Asperger Syndrome involves the restricted and stereotyped patterns of behavior, interests, and activities in which the individual engages. These features for some are compounded by communication problems. Individuals with this disorder have narrow interests that are all-absorbing (exclusion of other activities, a reliance on repetitiveness, rote understanding) (Gillberg 1997). Another feature is the imposition of routines and interest that may be on self or on others. Individuals may show a "severe impairment in social interaction and restricted, repetitive patterns of behavior, interests, and activities" (Cohen 1998, p. 11). Cohen goes on to say that although most show interest in making friends, their attempts to do so often are unsuccessful. One of the reasons these attempts fail is that these individuals will engage in "long-winded, one-sided conversations about their favorite interests while being insensitive to other people's feelings and nonverbal communication. Students with Asperger Syndrome seldom show interest in anything or anybody if it does not relate to themselves."

There are subtle impairments in three areas of development that often lead to inappropriate and sometimes disruptive behavior. The first area is social interaction, which may be characterized by social isolation that is not worrisome to the individual, distress caused by coping with the social demands of others, a lack of strategies for developing or sustaining friendships, difficulty picking up social cues, and socially inappropriate behavior. Young students with Asperger Syndrome do not actively seek the friendship or companionship of other students. When they are older, they may start to seek out friendships with others. Unfortunately, they lack the social skills necessary for developing such relationships (Cumine, Leach and Stevenson 1998).

A second area is social communication, which, among other things, causes difficulty with interpreting non-verbal communication (gestures, body language), difficulty interpreting different tones or the voices of others (e.g., anger, boredom), and understanding others in a literal way only. Students with Asperger Syndrome have great difficulty picking up social cues. When the teacher's face is red, and she is tapping her foot and frowning, these students may be the only ones in the class who don't recognize that the teacher is either angry and/or annoyed.

The third area that can affect behavior is social imagination and flexibility of thought. This is characterized by all absorbing interest, which peers find unusual, an insistence in certain routines, limited ability to think and play creatively, and difficulty transferring skills from one setting to another. The child has difficulty choosing and prioritizing (Cumine, Leach and Stevenson 1998). "The lack of negotiating skills, imagination and empathy in the child with Asperger Syndrome can be evidenced as an apparent 'extreme stubbornness'" (Cumine, Leach and Stevenson 1998, p. 63). Students become wedded to the routines of the day. If the physical education class begins at 10:15, at

10:16 they will become irritated and possibly agitated if the class has not started. These students often remind teachers of any abnormalities in the schedule.

Another feature of this disorder is motor clumsiness. Many children diagnosed with Asperger Syndrome show delayed motor development and have motor clumsiness that is reflected in difficulty developing such skills as riding a bicycle and catching a ball. They also may display awkwardness, or oddness in posture and gait (Klin and Volmar 1995). Additional characteristics are sensitivity to the close proximity of others, obsessional behavior and being particularly prone to stress (Cumine, Leach and Stevenson 1998).

Common behaviors may include: social ineptness; lack of understanding; a high stress level; lack of control over the environment; an obsessive and single-minded pursuit of a certain interest; and a defensive panic reaction (Myles and Southwick 1999). When these behaviors occur it frequently appears to be caused by a generalized inability to function in a world that the student finds unpredictable and threatening.

These students are emotionally immature, particularly between the ages of 9 and 19. They may be as much as one-third less mature as peers who are the same chronological age (Myles and Southwick 1999). Due to their seemingly strange social behavior, it comes as no surprise that these students are taunted and ostracized in school and, unfortunately, they are ill-equipped to deal with such teasing. They are aware that they are different from their peers and, consequently, experience problems of self-esteem, and self-deprecation. Their inability to learn social skills with a full understanding of their meaning and context presents social problems. They attempt to rigidly and broadly follow universal social rules, hoping to find structure in a world that often is confusing.

Some of the difficult behavior displayed by these students often is related to cognition and communication difficulties. This is particularly true when the student is in a stressful state. "When under stress the child reacts and does not think. The child may have a limited ability to place a thought barrier between impulse and action. The child may engage in rage behavior or blurt out inappropriate phrases because of this limited self-control under stress" (Myles and Southwick 1999, p. 5).

These individuals are susceptible to anxiety. "Any social contact can generate anxiety as to how to start, maintain, and end the activity and conversation. School becomes a social mine field . . . The natural changes in daily routines and expectations cause intense distress while certain sensory experiences can be unbearable. All these factors combine to make the person anxious" (Attwood 1998, p. 153). When students feel anxiety they may retreat into a special interest they possess. The more anxious the person feels the more intense the interest. "When anxious the person is also more rigid in their [sic] thought processes, and more insistent on routines. Thus, when anxious the person increases their [sic] expression of Aspergers Syndrome, yet when happy and relaxed one may have to be very skilled to recognize the signs" (Attwood 1998, p. 154). Part of the susceptibility for anxiety for students with Asperger syndrome is due to sensory processing issues. "Children with sensory processing difficulties are especially prone to extreme anxiety because it's more difficult for them to regulate, comprehend and operate in their social and physical worlds" (Baron-Cohen 2001, pp. 26-7).

* * * * * * * *

Case History No. 1

Abbie Snyder has been a public school teacher for more than 20 years. One year she worked with a 9-year-old boy, Joey, who had Asperger Syndrome. Joey was included in her regular education third-grade class, which had 28 students, six of which were identified by the Committee on Special Education and received special education services. Joey had a one-to-one aide assigned to him, received consultant teacher services from a special education teacher, and also received speech therapy. Snyder described her experiences working with him —

> *Joey looked like your typical average 9-year-old except that his motor skills were a little bit off. He was a little rigid. His balance was a little off. He was a very cute little boy who was often in his own little world. Joey could appear to be understanding everything you were saying or he might look like he was on task, but when you went to take a closer look at what was really happening, he had not a clue. You have to be really careful in a class with a lot of kids, not to overlook this. In instruc-*

181

tional situations, we had to move him so he wasn't facing a window. If he looked out the window he was gone. He was very distractible. In a situation where he was facing me, you could just tell that he would "glaze over." He would kind of focus above my head or something very small and minute on his desk might get his attention. He spent a lot of time tuning out. He loved comics. I think he went into a fantasy world. It seemed like he might be creating elaborate little movies in his head. Joey was in no way a classroom behavior problem in the typical sense. He was a manageable child, but you needed a one-to-one person to re-interpret directions and keep him on task.

Joey didn't initiate any real social exchange with me. He would respond with one-word answers if I actually pushed him. I would ask him questions to help him elaborate on what he was talking about. He sometimes did volunteer and raise his hand, and he would be really proud of himself. That hand would shoot right up there, and I was always careful to call on him. He didn't relate to the other kids. He seemed to want to, but he didn't really have the language skills to do it. He would talk about things that only interested him. He never asked other children about things that interested them. He often didn't relate at all. In the playground he would run up to other kids. He would do a strange hand motion near his head . . . flap a little bit. He would sometimes play chase games with the kids. I think he would get tired and didn't want to be chased anymore. He didn't know how to tell them to stop doing that or, they would tire of the game before he did. He would continue and that would annoy them. Then it would turn into a really negative situation for him.

Very often, for students with Asperger Syndrome, communication problems lead to problems with social interaction difficulty. This was true in Joey's case. Snyder explained —

Most of the kids didn't pay much attention to him. For some of them, quite frankly, it was like he was a piece of furniture. He was someone who was just there and they walked around him. They didn't really relate to him. If he was in a small group that was teacher-created, some of the kids would "mother" him. They would kind of take care of him and help him along. There were times where he was teased. I think that one of the characteristics of his disability was that he couldn't always tell when he was being teased. There was a very bright child in the class who was sometimes very mean and for whatever reason needed to put other people down. He was asking Joey questions like, "Are you toilet trained?" Joey, being who he is, answered very seriously, "Yes, I am toilet trained." This kid would repeat it and then a crowd of kids gathered and they were laughing at Joey. Since the other kids were laughing, the bright kid kept repeating the question, and Joey didn't understand what was happening. At some point he realized he was being laughed at. It hurt him, and he was very upset by it and he cried. He came in from lunch that day red-eyed and swollen-faced and really miserable. It was heartbreaking. So I talked to the other kid about the situation he had created for Joey.

* * * * * * * *

Since many students with Asperger Syndrome have interactional problems related to communication most often these students receive speech therapy.

Case History No. 2

Page Brooks is a speech pathologist who has more than 20 years of experience. For four years, she worked with a student, Benjamin, who was diagnosed with Asperger Syndrome. She started working with Benjamin when he was in kindergarten. Benjamin's behavior early on was more severe than Joey's behavior. Benjamin attended several small private schools, but is now in a fourth-grade regular classroom at a public school with a one-to-one aide as support. When he was younger some of his behavior included screaming, tantrumming, spitting, and stripping off his clothes. There were times when he needed to be physically restrained because he was kicking, and screaming and swearing. But Benjamin, like many individuals with Asperger Syndrome, has many strengths. Brooks reported that Benjamin was visual, mathematical, and extremely bright. He scored at a 17-year-old level when he was given a standardized test in third-grade. Benjamin, like Joey, had problems interacting with his peers. He often preferred to be by himself, but when he found a friend he had difficulty keeping appropriate boundaries. Brooks stated —

> *He had no friends in kindergarten, every-body knew he was different. As he got older the kids were kinder. Once, when he was older, he decided he liked a girl, but he went way to the extreme. He said he loved her, and we had to pull him off her on the playground because he went way too far. When she would "dare" to play with some-one else, it was a huge tantrum because for him it was, "How dare you . . . You are my best friend." He had a problem with exclu-sivity.*

Benjamin also had difficulty getting what he wanted because he didn't seem to know how to ask for things. Brooks elaborated —

185

> *At one of his [Benjamin's] schools there was a big hill where all the kids would go sledding at recess in the winter. Benjamin always would stand apart from the other children, but he would intently watch them sledding. When asked if he would like to go sledding he insisted that he would not. I assumed he wanted to go sledding also but didn't know how to ask. I worked with him on how to ask for a turn on the sled and within two days he was riding on the sled and reporting that it was his favorite thing to do.*

Brooks said, language problems contributed to Benjamin's frustration and lack of understanding —

> *He never got jokes. Jokes frustrated him as a matter of fact. He didn't like performing. He was very literal. I told him one day he had a frog in his throat and he got really mad at me.*

Brooks reported that Benjamin would engage in behavior that was atypical for most students —

> *He would say things . . . reminders to himself out loud like, "you need to pay attention and then look at the board." He would do this very quietly. It's almost like he would pull it from where it was filed. He had to hear it out loud. He couldn't just hear it in his head. I often wondered if he*

had a different tape playing in his head and that's why he had to say it out loud. I often thought he heard the tape playing in his head most of the time and that he was constantly battling against it.

Brooks noticed that Benjamin would appear confounded by his own behavior and often had negative feelings about himself —

Sometimes he would say to me, "I made the bad Benjamin come out. I made the devil Benjamin come out." He seemed sad.

There were specific triggers that would set him off, Brooks said —

The biggest trigger for him was getting something wrong. We worked on it being okay to be wrong. He did finally get that, but all he wanted was, "don't mark something wrong on the paper!" That's all he wanted. He was sharp enough to say to his teacher, "Just don't mark it on the paper." Unfortunately, his teacher didn't respect that. I was so proud of him when he articulated what he needed and then he got shot down. His teacher wouldn't even mark it on a separate piece of paper. That would have been okay with him. When something was marked wrong on his paper he would go off. I think anxiety is a big part of his disorder. I think he's anxious about being wrong and not getting it and what's going to be happening. Boredom was also a trigger for him. There were classes that were so boring to him, where he knew every single answer, and he couldn't stand sitting there being bored.

Benjamin had some very difficult times in school. According to his father, Benjamin was so depressed that he needed medication —

He was extremely unhappy, actually he was clinically depressed. He was on medication. They had no idea how to handle him. There was a lack of structure. His aide was inept. She would scream at him when he misbehaved. The last straw came when Benjamin told me one day that he had misbehaved and he said he went to time out. I was curious and asked "where do they put you in time out?" He told me, the bathroom. I called the director of the school and he confirmed that they used the bathroom for time out because there was no physical space in the building. I was upset that the director never told me about this. I told the director, "He's out of there right now!" I also was told that the director was pulling Benjamin's hair when he was misbehaved and needed to be restrained.

* * * * * * * *

Strategies

Consistency and structure are vital for students with Asperger Syndrome since they feel safer sticking to known procedures and routines. Presetting and preparation for transition periods and changes in routine will be extremely important. It is imperative that staff be as consistent as possible. Schedules and specific guidelines for task expectations greatly assist the student with Asperger Syndrome. Visual cues and graphic organizers are beneficial, as well, and academic and social expectations should be made as explicit as possible.

The student is more likely to interact with familiar people, so it is important to give that student the time to get to know the staff people. It also is important to try to avoid many changes in personnel. These students require a predictable environment. "The key words for intervention are routine, clarity and consistency. Minor environmental changes in the classroom, which simplify the organization and structure of the room and the tasks, can help the child make sense of expectations" (Cumine, Leach and Stevenson 1998, p. 34). To this end, the following aspects of a program should include the maximum consistency of approach. It is important to help the child understand what is expected by having clear, predictable routines. Introduce change gradually.

If the student becomes agitated, understand that the usual strategies for calming other students may have the opposite effect and make matters worse. Teaching stu-

189

dents to remove themselves to a safe place for stress relief will assist in decreasing serious behavioral eruptions and disruptions.

Strategies for dealing with anxiety can include, relaxation (which can be enhanced by listening to calming music), provision of a sanctuary without social or conversational interruption, use of massage, deep breathing, and thinking positive thoughts. Allowing the student to engage in a favorite interest also can help to distract and relax the student. "Another option is to encourage achievement by using the computer, going through school material that the person finds interesting and easy, and distracting the person by activities such as tidying up to restore order and symmetry" (Attwood 1998, p. 55).

Communication and social difficulties create a great need for teaching students with Asperger Syndrome positive interactional skills. Some aspects of social interaction that need to be taught are: first, and foremost, students need to know the basic social skills of listening and not interrupting. These students also need to learn how to take turns and share equipment. It is essential that instructions are clear and explicit. You cannot assume that the student will ascertain meaning from the context in which it is given. The student should be taught and assisted in identifying emotions and in learning how to read the emotional expressions of others. This would include physical, visual, and auditory expressions. It is important to teach students to discriminate between pretense and reality because they often miss subtle clues. The educator should assist these students in recognizing their ability to problem-solve and teach them visual and auditory strategies to promote self-reflection and recognition of self-experience. They need to be made aware of their thoughts, feelings, beliefs, and attitudes as well as the thoughts, feelings, beliefs, and attitudes of others. Avoid ambiguity by using visual cues to highlight meaning. Teach the student how to specifically make choices and build in opportunities for the child to generalize knowledge and skills (Cumine, Leach and Stevenson 1998).

The use of social stories has shown great promise in teaching students with Asperger Syndrome social skills. "Social stories and comic strip conversations were successfully used to teach social skills to a 14-year-old student with Asperger Syndrome. As a result of the training, the student's behavior changed. The student enjoyed using comic strip conversations and began to request their use from others at school and home" (Rogers, Franey and Smith 2001).

The educational staff should be aware of possible stress triggers and should take measures to reduce or prevent such triggers. There should be consistent breaks built into the student's program, to deal with stress. These breaks should be "a peaceful and relaxing time with no non-calming and non-welcoming stimulation. There should be no unnecessary touching, and the provision of gentle, quiet, steady, calming sounds" (Cumine, Leach and Stevenson 1998, p. 61).

Use a non-confrontational, objective and emotionally detached approach. "Cajoling, threatening and shows of emotion may lead to an increase in stress in the child, but not to cooperation. Calm, orderly and emotionally neutral approaches to negotiation with the child have the best chance of working" (Cumine, Leach and Stevenson 1998, p. 63).

"Very often the 'obsessions' that are found in children with Asperger Syndrome serve as hobbies, giving positive pleasure to the child. Rather than attempting to remove these completely, it is helpful to allow the child the 'hobby' under clearly recognized conditions" (Cumine, Leach and Stevenson 1998, p. 64). Place limits on attention to favorite activities, identify time and place of activity. Brooks actually was able to use Benjamin's strengths and interests to help him —

> *He knows every Beatles song . . . how many minutes and seconds it is and what album it's on. I took Beatles songs and I changed the lyrics like, (to the tune of "Hey Jude"), "Hey Benjamin, don't be afraid. If it's math time you can get through it." It worked, and we ended up with this whole book of lyrics that was designed for him. I said to him, "Now you can't sing that out loud because that would be weird and people would be mad at you, but sing them in your head." He remembered every lyric, so I was able to use an interest of his to help him.*

For specific difficulties Brooks used forms of behavior modification —

> *I used things like neutral countdown. "I'll give you 'till 10 and then, sorry, I gotta go." He would wait until I got to around*

six, five, four, and then when I got to about three he would be right there. He would say, "I'm ready. Don't go." Anything that didn't engage him in a verbal battle would work well. People who engaged him in a verbal battle inevitably lost. He was very verbal, very smart, and he was too good at it. We did a jar of good behavior. When he did something good we wrote it down and put it in the jar. When he felt bad I could say, "Look at the jar." The jar was stuffed with paper. The jar was visible and touchable. You could pick it up. You could look at it. It was wonderful and then he thought, "Oh, I am a good person. Look at all these good behaviors in the jar." Other kids bought into it and wrote things down on paper and put it in the jar like, "Benjamin shared his crayons." He would realize, "not only am I good, but other kids think that too because they wrote it down."

We used lots of social storybooks, but it couldn't be about him. I had to change it. I used to say, "I have this other boy who has this problem" and even though the problem was identical to Benjamin's problem, he bought it. I would say, "I need you to write a social story to help this boy solve his problem," and he would do it. You had to give him the script, but not personalize it to him. It wasn't important to him that look-

193

ing me in the eye would make me feel better. He couldn't get that. I just objectified it and made it a game. You lose a point if you're not looking at me. It created the habit of looking at me. Benjamin learned many of the social skills in a rote manner. He didn't do these things because they were the right things to do. He played the game and then these skills started to become automatic. We had an imaginary friend that worked well. It was a stuffed animal that he named the robo-monkey. Rather than coming from me, things would come from the wise robo-monkey. We had a whole book of things that the wise robo-monkey said. They were essentially social skills stories. Because they came from the wise robo-monkey, he bought it. I had to show him the whole range of emotions so that he would know what it would look like. I think that helped him.

Snyder also employed specific strategies while working with Joey —

I think it's helpful to teach proper responses. I think role-playing social situations is very important. What should you do when someone greets you? I think it has to be laid out for this type of child step by step. You can try to teach these kids how to have conversations. If you are with some-

one, you can ask him or her something about themselves instead of only talking about yourself. Of course, the role-playing would have to be entirely "scripted" at first, and modeled by typical peers, since a child with Asperger Syndrome is not going to come up with an appropriate response independently.

Many times students like Joey receive services to enhance programming. Coordinating these services can be difficult. It is essential that there is communication between everyone involved in the student's program. Snyder, as well as Joey, would have benefited greatly from better communication and coordination with other staff members. Snyder encountered problems while working with other staff members and saw a need for support and changes in other areas —

The one-to-one aide didn't really work out that well. There was really no one to supervise her. The consultant teacher didn't really come . . . maybe once in a while she would come in the room in an off-handed nonstructured way to say, "well hey, how are things going?" and then she'd leave. She wasn't really involved in his program at all. The speech teacher and I didn't really have time to talk too much about what was going on either. I would have liked some release time to get training where I could be trained, and given some

195

*idea of what kind of program this boy
needed, and what I could do as the classroom teacher to help him. I would have
liked some strategies for things that I could
do that would carry out what he needed
and not short-change the 27 other children
in the class.*

Brooks also offered the following suggestions —

*The best thing for a teacher to do is to lis-
ten when the kid tells you exactly what he
needs. Although there are rules, I think
there are ways to bend enough to honor
some requests. I think you have to be very
flexible. Routine, and knowing what will
happen next, are really important for these
kids. They need to know that this comes
after that and they have to see it. These students need to know what's happening and
when, and that helps them to know what to
talk about.*

Benjamin was able to make a great deal of progress,
Brooks said —

*When I met him in kindergarten he was so
classic. He was so different. Now I think
you'd be hard pressed to walk in and pick
him out. He's made great gains. It's absolutely incredible. In kindergarten he would
literally be in the corner, literally staring at
the wall, counting everything . . . counting*

the tiles, counting the calendar squares, counting anything that was countable. He didn't pay attention to the rules . . . didn't look at you when he talked to you. He was aversive to that. Today he's a wonderful conversationalist. He'll look right at you. He is still quite rigid, but not in a visible way. It comes out now in his opposition, where as before it came out in ways that were clearly physically deviant. He can be obstinate . . . "I don't want to do that. I don't like that. I'm bored with that. It's boring." Up until second-grade if he didn't know the answer with certainty, he would not give it a try. Guessing was not part of what he would do. He will now try to problem-solve. When he was younger, if I introduced any fantasy, he wouldn't buy it. He would say "that's false." We worked on that for a whole year. He can now imagine another planet and the planet grows candy canes. Now he's got several friends. He finally learned that it's okay to be friends with other friends. He did his first sleepover and was pretty successful. It was a remarkable step for him. He has learned that it's important to ask other people about what their interests are. He doesn't do it in a very natural way. He remembers that he's supposed to look at the other person, but it's not natural for him and he looks different when he's doing it, but he is doing it. He had a very flat affect early on, but he's learned to modulate better. In fact, sometimes he exaggerates. He still has a one-to-one aide, but the aide is now starting to fade into the background. He can now write a story using imagination. In kindergarten and first-grade he had a great deal of difficulty with imagination. He has gained figurative language.

As for Benjamin's future, Brooks speculates —

I think he'll be really successful. I think he'll choose a job that's got some solitude to it or where he could work by himself, like an architect or an engineer . . . something that uses math skills or science skills but that doesn't involve a whole lot of people skills. I think that's what he'll gravitate to. He'll need to learn how to de-stress himself. He'll have to play the right tape in his head to deal with stressful situations. He was the bright spot of my week. He was a challenge, but when it works you feel so good.

Benjamin's father attributes his son's success to several aspects he receives in his current educational setting —

The quality of the teachers is superb. The principal is very supportive. They understand what Benjamin's needs are. They picked the teachers that could work with him best. We were very deliberate about choosing the right aide. He's doing very, very well. He has a behavior plan where he gets a warning if he has a problem. After that, he has to write sentences and after the third thing, he gets pulled out. This year he's only had three warnings and that's it. He's never had to write sentences. All the problems were resolved very quickly. It used to be when he had a problem it would ruin the rest of the day. Now the behavior is corrected and he goes on and the rest of the day is fine. When you are in a public school you have more choices. There are more children to choose from for friends. This year he's friends with everybody. He has two really good buddies. In fact, he's had several sleepovers. He's just doing great and he's off all medication.

Benjamin appeared to me to be a bright boy who spoke in a fairly loud voice with an exaggerated inflection. Benjamin seemed distracted and was resistant to answering any question that would require a lengthy answer, and he seemed to have difficulty sustaining the conversation. The manner in which Benjamin spoke sounded somewhat precocious, but he also was quite charming, as apparent in the following Question and Answer forum:

199

* * * * * * * *

Q. Do you have any hobbies?

A. My hobby is playing sports like soccer.

Q. Are you good at soccer?

A. I am great and perfect at soccer. And now what is the next question, Barbara?

Q. Do you like school?

A. Yes.

Q. What's your favorite thing about school?

A. Now let's see . . . spelling!

Q. What don't you like about school?

A. Uhm . . . I have an aide who's way too firm with me.

Q. What do you mean he's too firm with you?

A. You know, sometimes I say something bad to myself, he says, "Benjamin, let's change that attitude or else."

Q. Have you tried to tell him not to do that?

A. Yes, but he says, "No, I'm fine the way I am." He's boring.

Q. What do you think of your teacher?

A. She is one nice young lady.

Q. What's the best thing your teacher does?

A. Have games like spelling challenge.

Q. What's that?

A. I don't want to describe it. It's too hard and complicated. What other questions do you have?

Q. If you could change something about your teacher, what would that be?

A. Nothing . . . I would change my aide to be really, really nice and not too firm.

Q. If you could have any aide, what would you want that aide to be like?

A. To be an angel most of the time, except if I had a big problem.

Q. What should the aide do if you have a big problem?

A. I don't really know. Maybe that's when he should be really firm.

Q. Do you get along well with the other kids in your class?

A. Yes, they're very nice young fellows.

Q. What's hard for you to do in school?

A. Usually I can't do math that well.

Q. What about sitting still for a long time, are you able to do that?

A. No! I always like to squirm around.

201

Q. Have you always liked your schools?

A. Yes, except the Smithers School. [The Smithers School is a small private school that Benjamin previously had attended.]

Q. What was that like?

A. It was like a wild zoo. Everyone was totally underestimating me. It was totally insane. I was very unhappy.

Q. If you were a teacher, what kind of teacher would you be if you were going to work with a kid like you?

A. Hmmm. I don't really know how to describe teaching at an elementary school. Could we skip that now?

Q. Benjamin, did you always have good behavior at the Green School? [The Green School is another small private school that Benjamin previously had attended.]

A. Not usually.

Q. What would happen?

A. I would get in big trouble and be sent to time-out.

Q. Is it easier for you to be better behaved at your new school?

A. Yes.

Q. Why do you think that is?

A. Uhm . . . because they have experienced teachers.

Q. Did you think that your teachers at the Green School had experience?

A. Yeah, but not good enough to handle me.

Q. Do you think the times you had trouble behaving was because you were bored?

A. Yeah, I was bored.

Q. When you're not bored, you don't have a problem?

A. Yeah, that's right.

Q. What is speech therapy like?

A. It was so wonderful. Ms. Brooks taught me all the stuff I wanted to learn.

Q. Do you know what you want to be when you grow up?

A. I want to go to college. Maybe I want to be an electrician for Nintendo.

Asperger Syndrome

Asperger Syndrome, is a Pervasive Developmental Disorder (PDD) characterized by severe and sustained impairment in social interaction, development of restricted and repetitive patterns of behavior, interests, and activities. These characteristics result in clinically significant impairment in social, occupational, or other important areas of functioning.

Characteristics:

Language:

- Speech is sometimes stilted and repetitive

- Voice tends to be flat and emotionless or exaggerated

- Conversations revolve around self

Cognition:

- Can be obsessed with complex topics (patterns, music, etc.)

- Eccentricity

- I.Q.: above normal in verbal, below normal in performance

- Many have dyslexia, writing and math difficulties

- Lack common sense
- Concrete thinking versus abstract thinking

Behavior:

- Movements tend to be clumsy and awkward
- Odd forms of self-stimulatory behavior
- Sensory problems
- Socially aware but, inappropriate reciprocal interaction
- Difficulty dealing with stress
- Low frustration tolerance
- Obsessive pursuit of certain interests
- Resistance to change of routine
- Defensive panic reactions
- Distractibility
- Inflexibility

Treatment/Intervention:

- Regular and organized routine
- Provide comprehension modifications
- Role-play social situations and social stories
- External scaffolding
- Set clear limits and follow through

- Teach multiple-solution generation
- Teach children how to respond to negativity
- Encourage extracurricular activities
- Behavior modification
- Provide breaks when student is stressed
- Self-esteem enhancement

Chapter Nine

Traumatic Brain Injury

Traumatic Brain Injury (TBI) is a unique disorder because the individual who suffers from this disability was previously healthy. A traumatic brain injury can have a devastating effect not only on the individual, but also on the entire family as well.

With increased advances in medical technology many more students are surviving traumatic brain injuries and are returning to school. Some of these students make full recoveries; others must adapt to a permanent disability that they will have to cope with for the rest of their lives.

Identification/Causes

Traumatic Brain Injury is defined by The National Head Injury Foundation as the following: "an insult to the brain, not of a degenerative or congenital nature, but caused by an external physical force that may produce a diminished or altered state of consciousness which results in impairment of cognitive abilities" (National Head Injury Foundation Task Force 1988, p. 2).

This definition can be broadened to include other causes of brain injury that affect students. "Acquired brain injury is an injury to the brain that has occurred since birth. It can be caused by an external physical force or by an internal occurrence. The term "acquired brain injury" refers to both traumatic brain injuries such as open- or closed-head injuries, and nontraumatic brain injuries, such as strokes and other vascular accidents, infectious diseases, anoxic injuries, metabolic disorders, and toxic products taken into the body through inhalation or ingestion. This term does not refer to brain injuries that are congenital or brain injuries caused by birth trauma. Acquired brain injuries result in total or partial functional disability or impairment that adversely affects educational performance" (Savage and Wolcott 1994, pp. 3-4).

The leading cause of TBI-related hospitalizations are motor vehicle accidents. The second leading cause of TBI- related hospitalization is falls. Firearms are the leading cause of TBI-related death (Thurman 2001).

Louisa Mangino is a special educator who has worked extensively with students who have TBI and with the families of these students. Mangino described an open-head injury as a brain injury that occurs when something actually penetrates the skull, such as a bullet wound or a knife. A closed-head injury can include swelling.

Unless the injury to the brain is moderate to severe, TBI in a student often goes undiagnosed. "Many children have no visible physical impairments after a head injury. Many of the subtle cognitive effects are extremely difficult to recognize, assess and remediate. It is this group of children who typically reenter a general classroom" (Tucker and Colson 1992, p. 198). It is quite common for students who have suffered a traumatic brain injury to be diagnosed as having Attention Deficit Hyperactivity Disorder, or other disorders that are associated with attentional difficulties. This creates a serious problem in terms of intervention. Students with Traumatic Brain Injury respond poorly to interventions that are typically designed for students with ADHD. In fact, these interventions can make situations much worse.

"The efforts to develop a classification of brain injury that will be helpful to the educator and parent must focus on the resulting impairments and disabilities rather than the mechanisms of injury" (Savage and Wolcott 1994, p. 5). Individuals who have TBI must be understood in terms of the specific injury incurred and the specific results of the injury.

Dr. Beulah Jaworski was a special education teacher for eight years, and worked as a behavioral consultant for seven years. Jaworski is currently a special education training specialist who works with educational staff members. In the course of her career, she said, she had worked with TBI students in her class —

> *Part of the problem is that we didn't always know if a student had a brain injury. One of the students I consulted with when I was a behavior consultant had a Traumatic Brain Injury that was caused by his father shooting him in the head. When I worked with him he was 14 and still had fragments of the bullet in his brain. He was charming, and people didn't know he had a brain injury. They thought he had a learning disability. He had extremely manipulative behaviors. After I did a paper chase, I saw*

*in his records that he had, indeed, suffered
a Traumatic Brain Injury.*

Characteristics: How School Performance and Behavior Are Affected

Unlike other disorders/disabilities discussed in this book, a student with TBI usually has led a normal life before suffering an insult to the brain. This makes life much more complicated and heartbreaking for these students. "This population is unique with respect to the suddenness of their injuries and the catastrophic changes and discontinuity brought about in their lives" (Deaton 1994, p. 266). "Although TBI children may seem to function much like children born with other handicapping conditions, it is different to be handicapped from birth than it is to acquire a severe disability in a second or two. Children with brain injuries may be able to remember how they were before their trauma, so a constellation of emotional and psychological problems not usually present in children with congenital disabilities becomes a valid concern" (Tucker and Colson 1992, p. 199).

TBI may have a significant impact on a child's ongoing development. Various risk factors have been found to predict outcome, but considerable variability remains unexplained (Anderson, Catroppa, Rosenfeld, Haritou, and Morse, 2000).

The emotional impact of a sudden disability can be great. "The loss of independence, self-confidence, and the comforting sense of invulnerability may result in adolescent withdrawal, depression, or rebellions" (Deaton 1995, p. 18).

Another frustration for these students is that physically many may look just like they did before their injury occurred. They may even achieve close to pre-injury cognitive levels, but they also may experience alarming behaviors that interfere with their ability to function appropriately in school (Tucker and Colson 1992). This can be confusing and disconcerting. In time, the reality that the abilities they possessed prior to the injury will not return causes many of these students to become withdrawn and depressed (Ylvisaker, Urbanczyk and Feeney 1992).

According to Mangino —

> *Every child who experiences a head injury will go through a grieving process. Of course, the grieving process will vary from student to student. Throughout the grieving process there's denial. There's acceptance. Some individuals will stay in that denial stage for a very long time. I don't believe that there are too many young adolescents that ever accept the injury. When you have a child that comes from a solid background and had high academic status it's hard for them when they come back from a head injury. This is particularly true if it's a subtle injury, meaning that they can walk and talk. They go through some emotional difficulty. Imagine looking in the mirror, looking the same way you did yesterday, but*

211

feeling totally different. The commonality among a lot of children is the feelings of guilt and blame. "Why did it happen to me? I must have been a bad individual for something like this to happen."

Students with Traumatic Brain Injury will be affected differently, depending on where in the brain the injury occurred. "The site of the injury, its severity, and extent of damage all help determine its effects" (Deaton 1990, p. 17). This can cause difficulty in planning and programming for these students. "Unlike any other type of injury, a brain injury can affect virtually any area of functioning, from those functions required to sustain life, to mobility, thought processes, language, emotions, and behavior" (p. 273).

Mangino concurs —

The results of an injury depends on where in the brain the injury occurs. However, it's not only where the injury occurs. The age of the child and the developmental stage the brain has achieved at the point of time when the injury occurred are also factors. Another important factor is the pre-morbid history. The pre-morbid history includes the following: Did that child come from a nurturing environment? Was there a behavioral problem previous to the injury? Did the child exhibit attention behaviors before or any sort of learning disability before the injury? This would be exacerbated after the injury. You have to take all of this into consideration.

It is not surprising that a significant number of individuals who are impulsive or have attention problems incur brain injuries. Impulsivity can lead to risk-taking behavior that is dangerous.

There is evidence that younger children with TBI display hyperactivity, attention deficits, and aggressiveness (Telzrow 1987). Older children demonstrate poor impulse control and difficulty in self-monitoring.

The effects of Traumatic Brain Injury can be quite varied. "A hallmark of brain injury is that the student's behavior after a brain injury can be extremely variable from one day or time of day to another . . ." (Deaton 1994, p. 259). "The acquired brain injury may result in mild, moderate, or severe impairments in one or more areas, including cognition; speech-language communication; memory; attention and concentration; reasoning; abstract thinking; problem-solving; sensory, perceptual, and motor abilities; psychosocial behavior; physical functions; and formation processing" (Savage and Wolcott 1994, p. 4).

It has been documented that most individuals with TBI will have difficulty with behavior. "For many, the most enduring, and potentially most incapacitating, effects of a brain injury are changes in behavior. Although no two persons with brain injuries experience precisely the same behavioral sequelae, behavioral difficulties are common" (Deaton 1995, p. 257). It is difficult to predict the specific behavior problems a student may have. There is no single pattern of disruptive behavior after brain injury in children. Behavior difficulties usually occur due

213

to the injury itself and due to the environmental interactions in which the child is involved (Deaton 1995).

Common behaviors of a child recovering from Traumatic Brain Injury include: confabulation, overestimating abilities, displays of inappropriate social behavior, low-impulse control, faulty reasoning, and the inability to initiate a desired behavior (Tucker and Colson 1992). In addition to these difficulties, cognitive deficits also are in evidence. These deficits interfere with the individual's ability to cope and cooperate, and often impede educational efforts.

Behavior problems in school increase due to the possibility of a change in temperament. Students with Traumatic Brain Injury often experience changes in expression of emotions, behavior, self-concept and interactions (Deaton 1995).

Personality changes also are common. The dramatic nature of these behaviors may produce feelings of anxiety and confusion in parents and teachers. This complicates home and school management (Barrin, Hanchett, Jacob and Scott 1985).

Other effects of the injury may include, "acting in socially inappropriate ways, irritability, increased emotionality, reduced judgment and motivation, perservation, lowered tolerance for frustration, and egocentricity seen through insensitivity to others, and an increase in demanding behavior" (Lehr 1990, p. 160). Some unique difficulties students with brain injury may have include: frequent inability to learn quickly from new experiences, need for repetition, need for increased structure and cues (Deaton 1994). Additionally, the abrupt loss of self-esteem and the need to establish a "new sense of self" also impacts behavior.

Mangino discussed particular behavioral issues that are specific to individuals who have suffered an injury in the frontal lobe area of the brain —

> *Many times children with a traumatic brain injury have a flat affect. The majority of the time, with a closed-head injury, you get frontal lobe dysfunction. The communication part, not the language per se, but the ability to read subtle visual cues, the ability to read social cues is affected. Many times I hear other teachers say, "the child is not motivated" or "the child doesn't initiate" or "the child doesn't organize." That's because of frontal dysfunction. They don't know how to go about initiating, organizing, and prioritizing. They seem to be unmotivated. These students can also appear to be stubborn, but it's not that they're stubborn. The problem is that they perseverate. What happens with frontal lobe dysfunction is that the child is on one track. They are unable to shift to another track. There are also sensory integration problems. The brain is not able to take so much information on, analyze it, and synthesize it. There may be highly aggressive behavior or changes in sexual behavior. Many times these students just refuse to do work. The older the child is the more we*

215

*see disobedience at home rather than at
school because they are more comfortable
at home.*

Some specific deficits related to closed-head injury
are: disorganized and impulsive thinking, language deficits, and deficits in concrete reasoning. Behavior problems result in difficulties in social judgment. These
students can display shallow moral thinking, impaired
insight, and impaired foresight (Feeny and Ylvisaker
1996).

Jaworski discussed specific behavioral difficulties
that can occur with students who have TBI —

*Probably at the very top of the list of
behavior difficulties is impulsivity. These
students have a great deal of trouble with
impulsivity. They also have a great deal of
trouble with executive function. They don't
seem to be able to read other people well.
They appear to be like a child who has a
very, very severe case of Attention Deficit
Disorder. They make bad choices and can
be very invasive of other people's space. A
couple of the children that I knew tended to
get involved in high-risk and dangerous
behavior. Some of these students get very
overwhelmed quickly by sensory things.
You have to assure that whatever environment they are in they have a way to get out
of it if they need to. Often if the student
with a Traumatic Brain Injury has a prob-*

> *lem, they can't seem to get back on track. If the student is thrown for a loop, it usually ruins the whole day for them. Additionally, these students have many social problems. One of the students I worked with would blow in your face if he couldn't get your attention. This type of behavior would set off other students. Then he would be ostracized. No one wanted to play with him and some of the students actively pushed him away.*

Sometimes students with TBI have difficulty processing information. This can cause them to have disturbing and dangerous behavior. Jaworski discussed one of her students who would become physically aggressive —

> *The very first student I ever taught with a brain injury had a subdural hematoma when he was two-months old. His mother had accidentally dropped him. He had violent reactions. This occurred when he was in situations that he found frightening or when he didn't feel safe.*

Strategies

Strategizing for the student with a brain injury requires a thorough understanding of what that student is cognitively and emotionally capable of doing. This is no easy task. "Because all learning is brain-based, injury to a child's brain may have a significant impact on educational, vocational, and social performance throughout life.

The brain is the student's 'learning machine,' and understanding how each student learns and what happens when learning does not take place has challenged educators for centuries" (Savage and Wolcott 1994, p. 5).

The National Center for Injury Prevention and Control offers several tips for individuals who are recovering from TBI. These strategies include: getting sufficient rest; not rushing back into daily activities, such as school or work; finding out when it is safe to resume certain activities, such as riding a bike; and, if able, writing things down that are hard to remember (The National Center for Injury Prevention and Control 2006).

Some effective strategies for assisting students with brain injuries include: having a routine daily schedule, having classes in the same room, and providing written lists and cues (Deaton 1994).

Several strategies for dealing with behavioral and cognitive difficulties include: plenty of reassurance and understanding of the specific needs of the student, as well as redirection of attention when necessary; verbal reminders of rules; provision of alternative ways to have needs met; pre-setting; demonstrations; shortening classes; provision of extra response time; review and summarizing; and, encouraging the student to ask questions (Tucker and Colson 1992).

When behavior problems are the result of cognitive impairment, cognitive remediation often is an effective route for addressing the deficits that cause or contribute to the behavior (Deaton 1994). Verbal rehearsal strategies have been effective for improving goal-directed behavior (Tucker and Colson 1992). Metacognition would have multiple benefits. (See Chapter Eleven for further information on metacognition.)

Many students with TBI have difficulty maintaining the attention necessary for learning and successful task completion. "Attentional problems are more easily managed through placement in small, highly structured classrooms, sometimes supplemented by pharmacological interventions" (Ewiing-Cobbs, Fletcher and Levin 1986, p. 64).

Some suggestions for intervention for students with behavior problems related to a Traumatic Brain Injury are: helping students gain self-awareness about their specific deficits related to their injury, including students in groups with other students who have TBI, teaching students appropriate behavior, and providing direct social skills training (Mira, Foster and Tyler 1992).

Disruptive behavior displayed by students with TBI can be disturbing, as well as dangerous. Some students, at times, can be extremely disruptive. Sometimes there are impairments in the brain that can cause students to lack inhibition causing an inability to self-monitor behavior. The student may say something sexually provocative or use inappropriate language. "For the injured child who refuses to respond to requests, possible strategies include providing written task instructions, rewards for task completion, time-out, removal to a less stressful situation, ignoring the noncompliance, loss of privileges or attention, giving more attention to cooperative students in the immediate environment, avoidance of frustrating situations" (Deaton 1994, p. 262).

219

Students with TBI decrease oppositional behavior when they are included in planning their own programs (Feeny and Ylvisaker 1996).

Counseling is a valuable and necessary tool in assisting the student with a brain injury, as well as assisting the student's family. "When behavior problems may be a manifestation of emotional reactions to a brain injury and its effects, individual and family therapy may be appropriate for dealing with the root cause of the behavior. This is most appropriate for the student with a brain injury whose memory and insight are at least somewhat spared" (Deaton 1994, p. 270). Group counseling in the areas of anger control and social skills also can be invaluable.

The following five intervention approaches in dealing with this specific disability may be helpful considering the many social skills deficits these students possess: traditional behavior management, behavioral approaches to teach social skills, metacognitive/social cognition approaches to enhance social skills, counseling, and atheoretic, specific skills approaches (Ylvisaker, Urbanczyk, and Feeney 1992).

Mangino discussed strategies and factors that are important when working with students who have TBI —

> *The most important thing occurs when the student transitions back to school, not only for the teacher, but also for all the team players. This would include the medical setting and educational setting. These people need to get together and learn what this child was like prior to the injury . . . the behavior, his likes and dislikes, his weak-*

nesses, his strengths. More importantly, before the student enters the program he has to be looked at holistically. So many times, emotionally, these students need support. I recommend a lot of counseling. I really think we need to address these issues and have the children speak to someone they can trust, but more importantly, someone who understands the process that they're going through. Then we can look at modification and curriculum.

The children who have a more severe injury really don't understand cause and effect. They need to understand the structure and they need to empower themselves. If a child has trouble acknowledging subtle social cues how are we going to teach him what's appropriate? We have to help these students develop self-awareness. We have to help them identify what makes them angry. We have to get them to identify the potential red flags that will get them to the point of no return . . . too much light, too much noise, a teacher. They need to develop self-confidence so that they can heal, because they're in this stretch where they don't know how to get out.

Communication with the family is very important. Many of the families also are going through a grieving process. Mangino said —

221

Often the parent feels it's a miracle that his child is still alive, but that same parent can end up with a lot of displaced anger toward the school or the teacher. If the schools and the teacher really communicate with the parents it usually helps. You have to make sure all the players are on the same team. It helps when the parents can learn about what is expected. They should go to professionals and not be afraid to go to support groups and have their children go to support groups. Parents need the knowledge and they need the support.

Jaworski also pointed out some specific classroom strategies that she felt were important when working with students —

I think that the key with any of these students is to look at the individual's profile. That's where you have to start. When a student re-enters the classroom, that individual should be tested every six months. The effects of the injury may decrease in time as they heal. After you do this, you have to then look at the classroom environment. It's important that these students have structure during the day. These students need to be able to use some sort of outside device to predict what's going to happen to them. I think many of the behavior issues came up because we forgot to pre-set them. The other students react badly toward them and then they react back. The teacher has to be really proactive and think way ahead. The teacher has to consider what might happen and then plan for it. If you do that, then I think you can program for most of those students in the general education class-room. Again, it's important that you plan ahead. A teacher who doesn't do that or who tends to be spontaneous is not the right teacher for a student with a Trau-matic Brain Injury.

[Students] need to have lots of support with the social stuff. Teaching social skills is very important and it has to be very spe-cific and scripted such as "when this . . . do this." We don't typically do this for most other children. When they are emotionally volatile you have to protect them from looking silly in front of people. We have to do a lot of teaching for the peers to help them understand what is going on with the student who has a Traumatic Brain Injury. This is particularly true for those students who knew the child before the injury. It's really helpful to involve the peers as soon as possible so that they can begin to root for the child. For the long haul, working on metacognitive skills is the way to go. This is what's going to carry them into their adult lives.

223

Jaworski also feels that it is vital for educators to be sensitive to the needs of the parents of students with TBI —

> *You also have to remember that the parents are very often dealing with a lot of guilt around their child's head injury. As an educator you can't blow that off. You have to be very sensitive to the issues that the parents bring to the situation. If you isolate yourself from what's going on with the parents you won't be successful.*

The full results of a Traumatic Brain Injury usually are not known immediately. Sometimes skills return to a student after several months. Some students can adapt and change their behavior after intervention. It is important to bring positive changes to the attention of the student. Videotaping at various intervals may provide for concrete comparisons between previous and current levels of functioning (Deaton 1994, p. 257). Encouragement and support are vital in helping students adjust to an unanticipated and unwanted change in their lives.

* * * * * * * *

Case History

Joey Romano is a charming, bright young man who is 20 years old. As a young boy he wanted to be a lawyer. When he was 10-years-old Joey was hit by a truck while riding his bike. The injuries he suffered were extensive; among them was a traumatic brain injury. Joey's older sister, Stephanie, is a special education teacher. She and Joey appeared to have genuine respect and love for each other, and an understanding of each other as apparent in the following Question and Answer forum with Joey and Stephanie.

Q. What do you remember about your accident?

A. Joey: Not much . . . just waking up. When I woke up I remember I called my brother and asked him where I was and why I was there.

Stephanie: He thought we put him there [in the hospital] because we didn't want him anymore and that we didn't love him. He didn't even know who we were.

Q. When did you start remembering what happened?

A. Joey: About three weeks after I woke up.

Q. Were you in a coma?

A. Joey: Yeah.

Stephanie: He was in a coma for about 10 days.

Q. How long were you in the hospital?

A. Joey: Including rehab . . . I was in the hospital six and a half weeks.

Q. How long were you out of school?

A. Joey: It happened in March and I was back in school by the end of May. Before I went back to school, I had a tutor who came to the house.

Q. When you went back in May were you ready to go back or do you think it was too soon?

A. Joey: I was ready to go back.

Q. What was it like going back to school?

A. Joey: It was real weird at first. It was hard getting used to the routine. For a while I didn't have that kind of routine. It was hard to adjust.

Q. What kind of a student were you before your accident?

A. Joey: I was a B student. I was a C or D student after the accident.

Q. Was it harder to do the schoolwork when you came back?

A. Joey: It was harder to concentrate and stay focused. Unless I was interested in it, I didn't want to do it.

Q. Did you have a problem with frustration?

A. Joey: Yeah, I was frustrated a lot. Kids made fun of my injuries. There were always kids picking on me because I couldn't play sports. I felt like an oddball.

Q. How were the teachers with you?

A. Joey: The ones that were concerned about me and liked me were real good about it. There were ones that weren't so great.

Q. What became hard about school?

A. Joey: Staying focused, concentrating and not thinking about other things. I wondered about why I couldn't play certain sports. My mind wasn't there. Sometimes I thought I couldn't do it. I would just get up and leave class for no apparent reason. It wasn't that I wasn't interested. I just wasn't there. They [the other students and the teacher] were somewhere in the class and I wasn't. I would just pack up my stuff and leave.

Q. Did you have any trouble understanding what your teachers were saying or what they were doing?

A. Joey: If I was interested in what they were saying and what I was learning about, no. If I got to class and it was boring, not that I didn't want to learn it, I might go somewhere else and then I found it difficult to understand. They would be talking in terms that I didn't understand. My motivation wasn't there. I couldn't push myself to do certain things.

Q. After your injury do you think your personality changed at all?

A. Joey: It's hard to say because I don't remember much before the accident. I don't remember being any different than I am now. I don't remember a lot of my childhood. I know things that happened because other people told me they did.

Q. Stephanie, do you think Joey's personality changed after his injury?

A. Stephanie: I think it did.

227

Q. Tell me how.

A. Stephanie: He was very sweet and innocent. After the accident he seemed to fly off the handle much easier. His temper and his judgment are different. When he was younger he could make a decision between right and wrong. After the accident he took more risks and wasn't thinking about what could happen. He became very active. He's got to always be moving. He never sits still to relax or calm down. He never takes a break. He's always moving. He's easily distracted.

Joey: I got sick of talking about my accident. It would make me angry and I would get into fights. Before my accident people could say stuff to me and I wouldn't care. After my accident, stuff would bother me. It got to a point where I could take so much. I'll start shaking and I'll get real nervous. Then I would think to myself that, "you better leave me alone or you're gonna get it."

Stephanie: Sometimes we would be talking to him about school. We'd ask, "what did you do in school today?" He would say "What the heck do you mean?" or he would just start screaming. So sometimes you couldn't even talk to him about certain things. It was like walking around on eggshells. Now I think he's getting better. He's learning to control his temper a little bit.

Q. After your injury what helped you?

A. Joey: Probably family and friends.

Q. In terms of your whole family what happened after the accident?

A. Stephanie: Oh, my God. That was the first time I saw my father cry. We honestly didn't know what was going to happen. My parents lived at the hospital for the six weeks he was there. My mother, I thought, was going to snap. You don't expect your son to die before you. I think as a family unit we became closer. My brother Frankie and I, after we would leave school, we'd go right out to see him. We were always there. We didn't want to eat. We didn't want to sleep. Once we knew he was okay and he came home my mother kind of let him slide on a lot of things. It was a miracle that he survived it. I think that had a lot to do with his behavior.

Q. What did you notice that was hard for your brother during this period of time?

A. Stephanie: It was hard for him to get used to getting back to a routine. He seemed to be struggling with the schoolwork. He was easily frustrated by it and he would shove it away. He was fighting a lot. He couldn't take the teasing. Someone would say, "What happened to your eye?" and boom he would knock you in the face. He also had trouble with organization. He still misplaces things. He's disorganized.

Q. When you came back to school, or at any other time during your school, experience what do you wish could have happened?

229

A. Joey: I guess that I wish I would have been treated differently and that I was more able to motivate myself.

Q. Do you think the school handled your injury as best as they could?

A. Joey: No.

Q. What do you think they should have done?

A. Joey: I should have had more time between classes. They had kids who would have tests read to them. I think I needed that and I kept asking them for that, but I never got it. I remember taking tests and sitting there unable to do it. I couldn't get focused. I was by myself and I'd look at the words and they would be a blur. I needed more support.

Q. Stephanie, as a special education teacher, what do you think the school could have or should have done?

A. Stephanie: He definitely needed more support. Joey needed attention and nurturing and understanding, and necessary modifications. They didn't do that at all. When he came back they treated him like they did before the accident, like nothing had happened. He wasn't able to concentrate, and when he got frustrated his teachers should have cued into it and told him, "Joey, don't worry about it. Meet with me after school. Mr. So and So can help you."

Joey: But instead it was always detention. I wouldn't go because I felt like I didn't do anything. I got frustrated doing the work, but there was a reason.

Q. Was there anyone in school you could talk to about all of this?

A. Joey: Yeah, I had a couple of teachers that were really good about it. My senior year I had to take journalism. That was a very frustrating class. Once a week you had to have an article written. In my town there was a company that was on strike. My teacher told me, "I want you to go there. I want you to videotape and interview people. Then I want you to write a report on what they said and what you think the outcome of this will be. That's gonna be your final exam." Everyone else had to take a written final. She modified that for me and that was real cool. She let me leave school to do this. I had another teacher who knew why I would fly off and why I would have trouble. I used to always go to his class. No matter what class I was in, he never minded. If he knew I needed to talk to him, he would talk to me. Even if I had a fight he would let me sit in the back of his class.

Q. Stephanie, what are things that are important for other educators to know about, concerning students with Traumatic Brain Injury?

A. Stephanie: They definitely should find out the background on the student, especially if they suspect that something is wrong. I mean if a student was genuinely a good student who had high grades and then they dropped right out, they should explore that and find out why. The teacher should definitely find out why. It could be from a childhood injury. As an educator you have to make that effort that will help your students, then you can see the reward and the benefit for the student.

Traumatic Brain Injury

Traumatic Brain Injury (TBI) is defined as an injury caused by an external physical force or by certain medical conditions such as stroke, encephalitis, aneurysm, anoxia, or brain tumors, with resulting impairments that adversely affect educational performance.

Characteristics:

Physical:

- Loss of motor control
- Seizures
- Sensory problems
- Impaired alertness and fatigue
- Speaking disorders
- Regulatory disturbances

Cognition:

- Attention and concentration difficulty
- Confusion
- Impaired planning ability
- Memory impairment
- Impaired communication
- Impaired abstraction and judgment

233

- Impaired ability to apply newly learned skills
- Lack of initiation

Behavior:

- Excessive agitation
- Extreme changes in emotion
- Disinhibition and impulsiveness
- Self-centeredness
- Loss of self-esteem
- Preservation
- Lack of motivation
- Low affect

Treatment/Intervention:

- Medication
- Redirection during emotional outburst (Don't dwell.)
- Metacognition
    - External scaffolding
    - Structure and consistency
    - Teaching organizational skills
    - Modifying curriculum
    - Provision of breaks when needed
    - Self-esteem enhancement

Chapter Ten

Attachment Disorder

As a teacher, the students I have had the most difficulty with were students who I suspected of having Attachment Disorder. I seemed unable to reach them. Building healthy, positive relationships with my students was always one of my strongest traits as a teacher. I often felt like a dismal failure when it came to working with these students. They appeared incapable of forming a relationship with me that was based on trust. This led to some disruptive and disturbing behavior.

Identification/Causes

Attachment Disorder, also known as Reactive Attachment Disorder, is defined by the Diagnostic Criteria from the *DSM-IV-TR* (2000) as a markedly disturbed and developmentally inappropriate social relatedness, in most contexts beginning before age 5.

Individuals with Attachment Disorder have an inability to form normal relationships with other people. Additionally, they have impaired social development and sociopathic behaviors due to the lack of secure attachment formation early in life (Wilson 2001).

Attachment Disorder is caused when a child fails to form an intense attachment to a parent. When this occurs

235

the child's developing sense of self is experienced as being bad and incomplete, and [his/her] autonomy develops on a very limited and fragmented manner (Hughes 1997, p. 1). Prolonged geographical separation of mother and child, without an adequate mother-substitute, during the first few years of life can lead to severe harmful effects (Bowlby 1952). Attachment Disorder behavior can include the failure to attach or positively respond to people, or indiscriminant attachment to multiple people, regardless of familiarity or caretaking function (Kronenberger and Meyers 1996, p. 482).

Reasons for a lack of attachment can include abandonment, abuse, or neglect. Sometimes a parent is unable to care for his or her child, as in the case of a parent who is abusing alcohol or drugs, or a parent who is suffering from a mental illness. Additionally, Attachment Disorder can be caused when a child is separated from the primary caregiver due to a prolonged illness of the child.

Adopted children are more likely to exhibit emotional, behavioral, and educational problems than children who are raised by biological parents (Kay Hall and Geher 2003). This is particularly true when children have been in orphanages and/or multiple foster care situations for a prolonged period of time. These situations may provide inadequate relationship building between a parent figure and the child. This makes the child more vulnerable to Attachment Disorder.

Although no research has been conducted on the influence of temperament on the development of Attachment Disorder, current knowledge suggests that temperament may play an important role in the cause of Attachment Disorder (Zeanah and Fox 2004).

The effects of Attachment Disorder can be serious, and, without adequate treatment, life-long. "The truth is that the damage caused by early neglect — or even by physically adequate but emotionally indifferent care — can be deeply intractable, not least because it may have neurological as well as psychological dimensions" (Talbot 1991, p. 30).

Characteristics: How School Performance and Behavior Are Affected

Typically children who do not have issues with attachment usually are comfortable interacting with others and they make those that they interact with feel comfortable. Interaction generally is reciprocal and emotions are expressed in a genuine manner. It appears that the children suffering from Attachment Disorder have a fear of getting close or just do not know how to get close. They seem to have an inability to love and trust, cannot make others feel comfortable, and, quite often, they suffer from depression.

Grace Carter is a social worker who has more than 20 years of experience working with students who have been labeled emotionally disturbed or behavior disordered. She works for a private agency that, among other services, provides residential and day treatment programs. Carter has worked as a staff clinician, supervisor, and clinical director and is now the associate director of a division of the agency. As part of her responsibilities she consults

237

with public schools throughout Massachusetts on how to set up and manage programs for emotionally disturbed and behavior-disordered students. Additionally, she consults on individual students. Carter says that about half the children she has worked with have had attachment issues. She feels this is primarily due to the fact that she has worked in residential treatment. Carter describes Attachment Disorder as a basic disruption of trust —

> *You are talking about children who are troubled and they are troubling to teach. These children don't fit into the typical classroom or parenting modality. School is really suited to a large group of children. The individualized attention that these kids need is really profound. They take huge resources. They take the emotional and physical resources of the teacher. They take the resources of other children. These students can look impulsive. They look angry. They can be aggressive and violent at times. They have control issues and control battles. There are power struggles. They have a constant need to be right. They lie about the obvious, and they know they're going to get caught. They cheat. They can have learning issues and language issues.*

According to the New England Institute for Attachment and Bonding some behaviors that might be displayed by these children are: an intense need to control others; a lack of authenticity; the use of affection as a tool to get something he or she wants, expressed on the child's terms, not the adult's; aggressiveness and apparent disregard about hurting others; lying, including senseless lying; and the inability to foster long-term friendships. Children with Attachment Disorder usually are unhappy and feel unworthy of joy. "These children are very likely to experience deep shame, intense rage, pervasive anxiety, and extreme isolation and despair. They also are likely to manipulate a variety of destructive and self-destructive symptoms whose functions are to attempt to make life bearable when it is lived outside the basic reality of interpersonal relatedness" (Hughes 1997, p. 1).

Bowlby documented the tendency toward shallow relations with adult figures and consequent impulsive, antisocial behavior, often seen in children who have been institutionalized for long periods of time, or who have been through a long series of numerous unsuccessful foster-home placements (1952).

Children with this disorder attempt to control all situations and often are described as manipulative and display disturbing behavior. ". . . this frantic control is manifested as constant oppositional and/or avoidant behaviors that represent their primary maladaptive means of trying to meet their developing autonomy needs" (Hughes 1997, p. 6). The child feels unsafe if he is not in control.

It is extremely difficult for an educator, or any other person, to form a positive relationship with these students. "When the child with a weak attachment interacts with a seemingly caring and giving adult, the child assumes that it is his own successful manipulation that is causing the adult to act in a caring way, rather than any nurturing quality of the adult or any intrinsic worth of the child. When the adult disciplines him, he interprets the discipline as abuse, rejection, and humiliation, further proof that caregivers are not to be trusted, and the need to rely on manipulative control of others becomes greater" (Hughes 1997, p. 4).

Some specific characteristics include: working hard to control all situations; relishing power struggles and the compulsion to win those struggles; causing emotional and sometimes physical pain to others; maintenance of a negative self-concept; avoidance of reciprocal fun; engagement and laughter; avoidance of asking for help or favors; avoidance of praise; avoidance of seeking love; and, deep feelings of shame (Hughes 1997).

Some children with Attachment Disorder will act up or will withdraw completely. They struggle to avoid or attract the teacher's attention and seem unable to share the teacher's attention with other students (Barnett and Trevitt 1992).

These students suffer from low self-esteem and have difficulty predicting their own behavior or the behavior of others (Hughes 1997; Barnett and Trevitt 1992). They have difficulty having and tolerating fun. They destroy their own things because of an "I'm not worth anything" attitude. They have difficulty learning, as well as playing. They interpret direction and appropriate discipline as rejection and often react in rage. They sometimes seek this negative reaction to confirm their feelings of inadequacy.

Children with Attachment Disorder have disrupted levels of cognitive as well as social engagement (Moss, St.

Laurent and Parent 1999). Metacognitive skills are under-developed due to a low-level of maternal structuring and a high-level of child off-task behavior. Metacognition involves, in part, an individual's ability to think about his thought processes in order to problem-solve. "In failing to provide an adequate cognitive or emotional framework for structuring joint activity, this interactive pattern may interfere with the development of auxiliary ego functions needed for both the development of self-regulatory and socioempathic skills" (Greenberg, Kusche and Speltz 1991).

Strategies

Dealing with students with Attachment Disorder can be quite frustrating, but "fixing" that student is an almost insurmountable feat. The damage can be intractable (Talbot 1998). One thing that is well-documented is the finding that if the individual with Attachment Disorder has any hope of improvement he will need intensive therapeutic interventions with active parent involvement.

Most children experiencing difficulty with attachment develop a controlling style of behavior designed to push others away. This protects the child from what he perceives as the possibility of more pain. Therapy involves breaking through the child's wall of distrust. It generally is held that unless this wall is broken down, the child will not be able to form a healthy interpersonal relationship, based on trust, with anyone. Intense therapy sessions should be implemented. "The therapy involves a great deal of physical contact between the child and the therapist and parent. During much of the most intense therapeutic work, the child is being touched or held by the therapist or parent. His intense emotions are received, accepted, and integrated into the self. With a therapeutic atmosphere based on attachment, he is able to begin to explore aspects of himself and his relationships with his parents that have previously not been accessible. The development of both the child's attachment to his parents and his integrated self is the primary goal of the therapist" (Hughes 1997, p. 7).

Students who show signs of Attachment Disorder need a comprehensive psychiatric assessment and individualized treatment plan. Treatment of this disorder involves both the student and the family. If there is no treatment, the effects of Attachment Disorder can permanently affect a student's social and emotional development (American Academy of Child and Adolescent Psychiatry 2002).

Carter feels the first place to start when working with students who have this disorder is to gather as much information about the individual student as possible —

> *As a teacher you have to think of the entire ecology of the student. If a change happens one place, it's going to happen everywhere. With a child with an attachment disorder, you need to know the child's history. These children usually have some trauma in their history. Trauma doesn't necessarily mean that they were abused or neglected. You can have a child with some mild, soft neurological issues that prevented him from attaching because of the way he was constitutionally. In any event, it helps the edu-*

cator to understand what the specific issues are surrounding the child.

Although the behavior of the students can be disturbing, it is essential that the educator be understanding. These children have to feel that the educator believes in their ability, can help them and are trying to understand them. "Be empathetic and open to a different way of perceiving the world; to be able to listen; to avoid collusion or being judgmental; to show a belief in the child and behave in a consistent manner that gives a message of accessibility" (Barnett and Trevitt 1992, p. 32). Building self-esteem should be an important aspect of an educational plan for students with Attachment Disorder. Carter concurs —

> *Self-esteem issues are always important. It helps to emphasize skills. You want to build self-esteem through the skills the student possesses.*

Working with these students who have major control issues can be extremely stressful for educators. Carter suggests some strategies for teachers to employ under these conditions —

> *Structure is really important and routine is really important, but nothing rigid. The teacher has to help the student gain control. You do this by giving them choices . . . but not too many choices. I think the key is that educators have to have their own feelings in check. You have to watch how you*

respond. Benign responses, I think, are very helpful. When a student says, "I'm not doing this assignment," it is important not to argue with that student. You can say, "Let me see if I can help you find some ways to do this assignment." When behavior gets really difficult the teacher cannot be afraid to ask for help. Children with Attachment Disorder can be such "button-pushers." Sometimes the teacher just has to walk away and let someone else take over.

The educator can play a part in helping the student deal with issues of anger and rejection. These students are unable to learn until they resolve such issues. Attention must be paid to the state of mind and feelings of these children. If not, their cognitive learning is unlikely to move forward. "One of our tasks is to put the children in touch with this pain, particularly that relating to loss, until they are ready to contemplate the future and the renewal of their appetite for learning. The use of the metaphor in creative work and the use of educational materials enable them to express some of their feelings within the safe boundaries of the material" (Barnett and Trevitt 1992, p. 25). Allowing these students to regress and engage in activities that seem immature can assist them in coming to terms with who they are.

Students with Attachment Disorder do better in school when they have a space of their own in which to work with a trusted adult. They also do better with individual attention or working in a small group (Barnett and Trevitt 1992).

Transitions and changes of routine are particularly difficult. Students making the transition from elementary to secondary school may require one adult to oversee all of the different teachers with whom the student will interact. The overseer can instill trust and prevent some manipulation (Barnett and Trevitt 1992).

It also is important to communicate and work with the parents of these students, Carter stressed —

> *The connection between home and school is key. You may be dealing with parents whose resources are limited. Their life circumstances can be troubled. Some parents are really vulnerable and intimidated by the educator's relationship with their child. As a teacher you have the child for nine months. The parents have them for the rest of their lives. Keeping constant communication is key. When the educator feels communication is breaking down, or there are issues of anger or conflict, work through it. Don't give up. Keep up the relationship with the parents because it is in the best interest of the child. If you can bring other people in to help you with that process, do that. Building a relationship with parents enables you to get releases of information to be able to talk directly to a treating therapist or an after-school provider who may assist you in working with that student. This is true not just for the social worker but for the teacher as well. You need to*

communicate with the providers for the student so that you can get support and give support. Psychiatrists, psychologists, and social workers often have to treat individuals without getting direct information from teachers. They may get this information indirectly, but it's not always accurate. If you don't have a positive relationship with a parent, you are never going to get that information.

Bill Murphy is a school social worker who works for a school designed for middle school and high school students who display highly disruptive, disturbing, and dangerous behavior. School districts that are unable to deal with the intensity of this level of behavior refer students to this program. Many of the students Murphy works with have Attachment Disorder —

The kids that I work with are mostly 16-, 17- and 18-year-old kids. They are very guarded, very reluctant to talk. They're very defensive and actually spend much energy pushing you away. They're going to try and push you away . . . like "here's someone who's trying to get close to me." They don't attach. They respond with, "I don't want to get into this nurturing thing. You're trying to be nurturing with me and I don't want that." So that's one of the things that I tuck in the back of my mind. These students are very defensive. They're very guarded. Their armor is always up there. They're trying to protect themselves. You have to go really slow with these students.

* * * * * * * *

Case History

Scott was one of Murphy's students. Scott's mother was a drug user who neglected and abused him during the first five months of his life. This student was resistive and hostile toward Murphy, which is typical for students with Attachment Disorder. It was a slow and somewhat painful process trying to engage with this student, Murphy said —

> *The first week I met Scott I was kind of introducing myself . . . explaining that I was a social worker in the program . . . and "this is the way I do social work and how would you like to meet?" [Mr. Murphy was referring to meeting for social work sessions.] As I was talking to this boy he averted his eyes. There wasn't any eye contact. He said, "Meet with you? . . . never. I never want to meet with you." Scott wouldn't even put his head up . . . unwilling to make eye contact with me. This seems to be a sign of someone who has Attachment Disorder . . . not only are they not interested in talking with you, but they're pushing you away. You can feel the anxiety in the room go up when you start to*

*try and get close to one of these kids. So
you kind of have to meet the kid where he's
at. I told Scott that it was okay that he
didn't want to meet with me and that I'd
check in with him later sometime. I kind of
let students like Scott get a feel for me first
before I proceed. I know they'll see my face
often. I might come into their classroom
and some other kids in the program will
say, "Oh Bill, you're gonna meet with me?"
and they'll go out of there with me and the
kid [student with Attachment Disorder]
may see that it's okay, "Joe thinks that
Bill's okay," and he tucks that away and
sees that after a few weeks in the program,
"okay he's part of the program." That student may also think, "He doesn't seem too
threatening. He doesn't seem to be too
intrusive. Kids seem to think he's okay."
Then maybe a few weeks into the program
he may go with me.*

Scott often attempted to challenge Murphy's authority —

*With Scott . . . he was testing me. He
would start doing some stuff, and I think it
was sub-conscious on his part . . . or else
he was just kind of brilliant in the way he
tested me. He would do something that I
had to set a limit with. In my job, I sometimes have to cover for a teacher who is
out of the room. I was in there [Scott's*

classroom] covering for the teacher and he was throwing stuff and then filling up these exam gloves with water . . . like making water balloons out of exam gloves and throwing them. So I had to set a limit and actually bring him to time-out. I did that, and Scott started shouting at me. He was just being extremely disrespectful to me and calling me every name in the book. He was being obscene, and he was good at it. The things he was saying about my mother were really starting to get under my skin. He was pushing my buttons. I think he was just seeing how I was going to react. He was pushing me away and really trying to make it so I didn't like him. He had radar. He went right to some of my issues and knew how to get under my skin. He knew how to push my buttons. I think the test was, "How is Bill going to react to this?" I came back the next day and just sort of picked up from there and just moved on and didn't hold that against him . . . didn't make an issue of it . . . didn't do a lot of processing about it because I didn't think he was ready or would have been able to do it. I was using my gut and I didn't process with him because I believed it just would have escalated him.

249

Murphy used specific strategies —

I believe that behavior modification isn't always effective with these guys because you don't know what the reinforcers are, especially if the reinforcer is to push your buttons or to dismantle your program. I think establishing that trust and rapport is something that you have to earn, and these kids are very intuitive. They're going to test you and push you away because it's very scary for them to risk being detached again, for lack of a better word. To run the risk of letting somebody in, and then losing that person again, is so not okay with them that they will keep you away at all lengths, so you have to prove that you are in there and you're gonna hang in there and accept them for who they are. What I think is helpful is some of the Rogerian stuff . . . the unconditional positive regard . . . meeting them where they're at. You have to convey a kind of acceptance of this is where the student is, not condoning the behavior, but just understanding that's where they're at and move on from there. If you're angry with a kid with Attachment Disorder, you've lost him. Yet, on the other hand, if you're not direct and confrontative . . . if you're weak in some ways . . . if they perceive weakness or if they perceive that you're gonna be wishy-washy and you're not going to address the hard issues, you've lost them too. You've lost their respect. It's like a tightrope. You need to be able to treat them with respect, convey empathy and also confront the dysfunction.

Eventually Murphy was able to make headway with this student. Engagement came due to an unexpected situation —

I think I passed the test with this kid because he saw that I was back there the next day. I wasn't judging him and I wasn't putting anymore expectations on him, but I was still making myself available to him . . . you know, checking in on him . . . simple things like just asking him how he was doing . . . seemingly superficial, social kinds of things. I would say, "Scott, how are you? Did you do anything this weekend? Did you have any fun?" And it would always be . . . the expressions on his face were always like I was something he had scraped off his shoe. He was telling me, "Who are you? Don't talk to me." But I would hang in there with him. I would leave it at that. I wouldn't make issue with his inappropriate response to me and I would just say, "Okay, I'll catch you later" and go on about my day. He would continue to see me with the other kids. It came to a point where Scott's attendance started

251

to become a problem. Eventually we needed to file a PINS [Person In Need of Supervision] for his attendance. That really put me in the bad-guy seat, but ironically it's where things turned around with him. When I did this it must have registered in his mind that "even though I'm pushing Bill away he still is making sure I do what I need to do. He cares enough that even though I'm really being obnoxious to him and this is going to make things worse, he's doing it anyway." It was unexpected from my perspective that he would actually start to get closer to me at this point. After that, Scott started to talk to me about the things he likes to do. He would talk to me about his BMX bike and he would talk to me about something he was going to do that weekend. As things progressed he was able to continue to talk about things and actually got into a little bit more meaty kind of things. Kind of like peeling the layers of the onion back. It was safe for me to be just on the very surface of his life.

Colleen James is a special education teacher who has worked with Scott for a year and a half. James said —

Scott presents himself as a very mature person on the outside. He may walk down the hall in a strong manner . . . stand up tall and walk with great confidence, how-

ever, when there is any sort of engagement, whether it's positive or negative, Scott may revert back to being very childish. Whenever there is any discussion about family he gets very edgy. He literally jumps off furniture or off walls. If you were to touch him, he becomes very jumpy. He is constantly defensive and on guard. He lashes out. It has taken a long time to build any sort of trust and the trust that we have is very superficial. There are times that he knows we'll help him out so he'll come around and seek us out. Scott always has ailments. He says he's sick, and he has to go home and it has to happen right now. As soon as we nurture him you can see a factor of him wanting us to be there and at the same time he's pushing us away. There's a real pull and push action. He has increased his work production. Originally he wouldn't do anything. He has no self-esteem when it comes to schoolwork. However, certain staff members are able to work with him and certain staff can motivate him. It's up for grabs what days he'll work and what days he won't. Scott refuses to go to therapy, and his mother refuses to go to therapy. When you see the interaction between his mom and him it's playfulness, yet they're pushing each other away at the same time. There seems to be no true bond.

> *There's no bond where he trusts her and she trusts him.*

James said she noticed regressive behavior when Scott felt insecure or threatened —

> *He's very physical. He might grab something and throw it. He might throw his body against a wall, a door or he might kick something. He yells out. You can see in his whole affect that he becomes a little boy. Here he gorges on food that anyone will give him . . . if it's given through the school. He's a little bit scared to take stuff from anyone else. I think he feels that he needs to control all situations, but he doesn't want to. This creates a lot of stress for him. He constantly says he wants to run away. When you give him positive feedback he sometimes has to push you away. I think it's because he's afraid he's going to get hurt. He overreacts to almost every situation so that he doesn't have to feel close or feel good. His always having ailments is a way of protecting himself too. He can't feel too good.*

James described some the strategies used to help Scott in the classroom —

> *Scott needs to feel that we are on his side. We try to show Scott that even when you jump off of our walls and you try and hang*

from the ceiling . . . literally, the next day we start over. I think that with all this time we've put into working with Scott he trusts us more. He seems superficial with his trust, and I think that's because he doesn't know if he wants to trust us because he is afraid of losing it. He's not really sure what's going to happen with it. I don't ask him to work with other students. When he's in a certain mood I give him a lot of space. I think that he needs that. When he approaches me that works best as opposed to me approaching him. Approaching him, even with something very simple might bring him into a full-fledged rage because he doesn't want anybody close to him at that moment. Sometimes we let him run around a little bit. I think he sometimes feels confined. He's climbed out of the window many times. It's almost like he can't breathe. He's scared that people are too close.

Attachment Disorder

Attachment Disorder is developed when children, for different reasons (neglect, abuse, separation from caregiver, etc.) do not form a trusting bond in infancy and early childhood. A lack of trust generates feelings of aloneness, being different, pervasive anger, and an inordinate need for control. These children do not seem to know how to have fun and often have difficulty learning. A trusting bond is essential in continued personality and conscience development, and serves as the foundation for future intimate relationships.

Characteristics:

- Superficially engaging and "charming"
- Lack of eye contact
- Indiscriminately affectionate with strangers
- Destructive to self, others, and material things
- Cruel to animals
- Stealing
- Lying about the obvious
- No impulse control
- Learning lags
- Lack of cause and effect thinking
- Lack of conscience
- Abnormal eating patterns

- Poor peer relationships
- Preoccupation with fire
- Persistent nonsense questions
- Incessant talking
- Inappropriately demanding and clingy
- Abnormal speech patterns
- Sexual acting out

Treatment/Intervention

- Intensive individual and family counseling
- Empathy and compassion
- Teach children to take responsibility
- Set clear limits and follow through
- Try not to engage in power struggles
- Maintain a low-key but firm stance
- Teacher must be consistent and accessible
- Child must feel secure in the environment

Chapter Eleven

Behavior Interventions

Perhaps the most critical piece in dealing with disruptive behavior is not the actual behavior displayed by a disruptive child, but the reaction to that behavior by the educational staff and parents. As educators and parents, we have the ability to de-escalate a problem, and we, unfortunately, also have the ability to escalate the problem. It is important for educators or any other adults to stay calm and in control.

One of the most potent tools of good behavior management is having a positive relationship with the child. The better the relationship between the child and adult, the more motivated the child will feel. When this occurs the child is much more likely to be cooperative and appropriate. "When children feel that you value and care for them as individuals they are more willing to comply with your wishes" (Boynton and Boynton 2005, p. 6).

It is always a good idea to include the child in programming and/or any intervention plans. Theorists have maintained that children are empowered when they are able to make meaningful choices about the way they spend their time (Hewes 2001). When children have legitimate and appropriate power they don't have to seek illegitimate and inappropriate power, which often is the cause of problem behavior. By building choice into the environment you provide children with appropriate opportunities to make their own decisions (Kaiser and Sklar Raminsky 2003).

Sometimes having a thorough knowledge of the individual student and the student's disability is simply not enough to help that student be successful in the classroom and school. This is true even if we have a classroom and school environment that is conducive to academic growth and positive social interaction. Some of these students still will have a great deal of behavior difficulties and will require additional support. Creating a specific behavior intervention plan is one form of support.

The design of the behavior intervention plan (BIP) should be based on a functional analysis of the behavior and on the hypothesis derived from that analysis. The most important information to be learned from the analysis is what the function of that behavior is or what the students are communicating to us by their behavior.

An analysis of the antecedents, behavior, and consequences (ABCs) of specific behavior yields information that leads to a hypothesis about why the behavior is occurring and how to deal with it.

Antecedents are the specific setting in which a behavior occurs. To identify the antecedents, the following questions must be answered:

- Who is present when the behavior occurs?

- What is going on when the behavior occurs?

- When does the behavior tend to occur?

- When does the behavior tend not to occur?

- Where does the behavior tend to occur?

- Where does the behavior tend not to occur?

Specific antecedents could be, but are not limited to: who the individual is sitting next to, hunger, temperature of the room, and subject being taught.

Consequences of behavior are actions that usually follow the behavior in that setting. To identify the consequences the following questions must be answered:

- What happens after the behavior occurs?

- What does the staff do?

- What do the other students do?

- What does the individual who engaged in the behavior do?

- What do you think increases the likelihood of the behavior occurring again?

Specific consequences could be, but are not limited to: a teacher's anger, being sent out of the room, or other students laughing. Once a functional analysis/assessment is performed, a behavior intervention plan suited to the individual can be developed and formulated (Zimmerman 2007).

A team approach to answering these questions is the best way to get the necessary information. The team should include teachers, teacher aides, parents, the individual student, administrators, social workers, psychologists, and anyone else who knows the student well. When this information is known to the educational staff, an appropriate behavior intervention plan can be put into

261

place. Members of the educational team, including the student, should be assigned specific responsibilities in order to carry out the plan consistently.

It is essential that any interventions should be considered therapeutic and not punitive. Interventions must have as their major function, improvement in the quality of the student's life. There certainly are many ways to stop inappropriate behavior, but if the method used causes any damage to the student it should cease immediately.

It also is important that students aren't asked to do things they are physically or emotionally unable to do (e.g., asking a student with Tourette Syndrome to stop facial tics or asking a student with Attention Deficit Hyperactivity Disorder to sit for hours working on a tedious assignment).

The use of medication to assist a student in controlling behavior is, to say the least, controversial. There are no easy answers to the question of whether using medications is good or bad. As with any intervention, using medication must be decided on a case-by-case basis. "It's difficult to prescribe for a young child and not feel some reservations about putting chemicals into that tiny body. At the same time, when I see the dramatic improvement, the diminished aggression and frustration, the happier child, I end up saying, 'If that were my child, I would want him to have this medication'" (Waldron 2000, p. 14 quoting John M. Talmage, MD).

If a physician recommends medication for a child, it is the family's decision of whether or not to medicate their child. It is not surprising that parents often are hesitant when it comes to putting their child on medication. Educators should not aggressively push parents to make that decision. Gentle and supportive advice is much more effective. An educator should never make a recommendation that a student be put on medication. Educators are not qualified to make such recommendations. If an educator feels that a child might benefit from the use of medication, he can recommend that the parent bring the child to the family physician for an evaluation. If a student is put on medication, educators should observe the student closely and note any adverse changes in that student's behavior, such as drastic changes in mood, lethargy, anxiety, hyperactivity, or physical discomfort.

If the correct course of action is to give a student medication, one must consider other interventions in addition to the medication. Teaching the student strategies to cope with daily life is essential. The student must be reminded that the medication does not make him a better, nicer, or kinder person, it merely allows the student to access his potential.

The ultimate goal is to make all students, no matter what disability they have, as independent as possible. To this end, a plan for ceasing intervention should be included in a BIP. Eventually, the students will have to assume the role and responsibility of monitoring their plans. This, indeed, may be the most important part of any behavior management plan.

Consistency, structure, and flexibility are essential for any behavior plan to work. (This is discussed extensively in Chapter Three.) Other essential elements for behavior plans include the following:

263

Communication

Students with disabilities and behavior problems are hypersensitive to criticism and often misinterpret what is said as being a rejection. For this reason, it is important to be aware of the way you are talking and communicating with these students, whether it is criticism or not. Keep instructions simple and direct.

One of the most important features of good communication is having good listening skills (Zimmerman 2007). Kauffman (2001) states that "Teachers will not be successful unless they learn to listen skillfully, and to watch students' behavior with understanding. Youngsters who do not believe they are being listened to will go to extreme lengths to make themselves understood, often getting into additional trouble by their efforts to establish communication" (p. 536).

Many students with disabilities and behavior problems who engage in disruptive actions may be unaware of their behavior or unaware that the behavior is disruptive. Attempting to verbally respond constantly to all of these disruptions, the teacher would be talking quite a bit and the response would be interpreted as nagging. For students with disabilities and behavior problems, it is likely that the only verbal recognition that student would receive would be for disruptive behavior. Of course this doesn't mean to ignore such disruptions. Instead, whenever possible, use non-verbal cues. A tactile message such as a hand on the shoulder works well with some students. Sometimes visual signals such as a wink also work well. I worked out a series of private visual prompts with some of my students; no one else in the class knew about them. For example, when I rubbed my temples it signaled to a particular student that he was drumming on his desk and that I wished him to stop. Since it is nonverbal, this prompt can be done without the need for the teacher to stop instruction (Zimmerman 2007).

When verbal cues are needed, go directly over to the student. Do not give directions or re-direct students from across the room. Administrate consequences in a calm manner. Getting angry, yelling, or humiliating students with behavior problems will almost always have a negative impact on the situation. The student could become confrontational or hostile in an effort to "save face" in front of peers.

It is extremely important when communicating with students to avoid humiliation. Humiliation will only make the situation worse. It often creates resentment in a student's mind and that student will often seek revenge. In the same vein, adults should never use sarcasm. Sarcasm is not humor and also causes resentment. "Sarcasm is dangerous, cruel, and unprofessional and should never be used in schools" (Boynton and Boynton 2005, p. 93).

Academic Modifications

Most students who have disabilities and behavioral difficulties have difficulty learning in traditional ways. As a result, many of these students will require numerous academic modifications, although some may not require any at all. Often when a student's academic program is modified the student's behavior improves dramatically.

265

Academic modifications should be tailored to meet the needs of the individual student. Modifying appropriately can be a difficult task. It is important not to modify or "fix anything that's not broken." Providing a crutch when it is not needed may cause students to believe they are worse off than they actually are. Conversely, if modifications are not extensive enough, the student often becomes frustrated and angry. This in and of itself can create behavioral difficulties in a student who, up until this time, had none. The following are some suggested academic modifications that I have used in my classroom or have suggested to others. I have broken them down into specific categories of academic areas.

External Scaffolding

Most people consistently organize thoughts and plans of action internally. An average child usually understands and follows the morning routine before a school day without needing a checklist in a written form. Information about the routine is stored in the child's memory and when he wakes up he does the things he needs to do (eat breakfast, brush teeth, comb hair, get books ready, etc.) and then he mentally checks off these tasks. For some students with disabilities, waking up in the morning can be a nightmare as the student feels overwhelmed and doesn't even know where to begin. This lack of internal structure also can cause a tremendous amount of frustration that may create a situation in which the student shuts down. Imagine waking up like this every day! Being prepared for the events of the school day and then living through the school day can be extremely difficult. The student sometimes can have one disaster followed by another and feel completely overwhelmed and inadequate. It is for these reasons that the student needs help in developing an "external scaffold." The external scaffold replaces, or at least compensates to some degree, for the student's inability to organize internally. Some students need just a light framework because they are able to organize some things internally yet others will require a great deal more. As the student begins to internalize some of the routines and responsibilities, the scaffolding can be reduced. For some students, however, this will be a life-long battle and they will require this scaffolding forever. Some strategies for creating external scaffolding are:

1. **Teach the student how to make a list and how to follow it.** People sometimes take for granted that making a list is easy while students with disabilities and behavior problems have difficulty with this task and with following through. Start small (no more than two or three simple tasks on a list) and then work your way up to longer and more complicated lists. It may help to start by having the student create a list for a schedule he already knows and follows.

2. **It is important that students with disabilities understand and know how to follow a schedule.** If you need to, start with an hourly schedule then work up to daily, weekly, and monthly schedules. Students with disabilities are notorious for

asking, "What time is lunch?" at 8:30 in the morning. To these students it is a legitimate and sincere question, related to their poor sense of time. It is essential for success, in the present as well as in the future, for students with disabilities to use calendars, clocks, and schedules as tools to help them follow the routines. A schedule taped to a student's desk can be very helpful. Students who have not yet learned to tell time will need a schedule with times and their representations on clock faces. Being able to follow schedules alleviates much of the stress that people with disabilities have. They are aware of what is coming up and there are fewer surprises. I find my schedule book, with its calendar, an extreme source of comfort, and I am most unhappy and anxious without it. I take it everywhere.

3. **Use a homework assignment chart and a classwork assignment chart.** At first, filling out the chart will be the responsibility of both the student and the educational staff, but eventually the student should take over the responsibility. Students will differ in terms of how long it will take before they can assume this responsibility themselves.

4. **Provide a binder that has several organized sections for work to be done, homework assignment charts and completed assignments.** It also should contain daily and weekly schedules, and the names of people (where and when to find them) to contact when there are problems. Color-coordinate the binders for easy access and insist that the student carry the binder with him at all times. Recognize that for a significant time period after establishing the folder system, adult cueing will be necessary to keep up with the folder(s).

5. **Provide a set of materials to be used in the classroom and a set of materials that will be kept and used at home.** Materials should include a writing implement, paper, and any books the student may need. Emphasize that the materials used in school should not leave the classroom and the materials used at home should not leave the house. Many students with disabilities are disorganized and disheveled. They have difficulty holding onto and transporting materials. This does not signal a lack of respect for materials, but an inability to remain focused on the possession of the materials.

6. **It will be useful to break up larger assignments or projects into smaller**

269

components with specific deadlines for each component. Not only does this make a larger task less overwhelming, it provides a road map for tackling the project.

7. **Teach a student with disabilities and behavior problems how to ask questions and make comments appropriately.** So often a thought or question pops into the student's head and he immediately shouts it out. Instruct by modeling what to do when you have a question or comment. (It is not a good idea, for example, to talk about how the puppy ripped up the couch in the middle of a science lesson.) The student needs to be told this and told what to do if he has a question or comment at an inopportune time. Suggest that the student write down the question for later, or if a tape recorder is available, to quietly tape the question. Keep in mind that one reason students with disabilities and behavior problems shout out is that they know if they wait, they may forget their comment or question. In any event, there should be consequences for students when they inappropriately blurt out things, and there should be consequences when they successfully have controlled themselves. As previously stated, it is always important to reinforce appropriate behavior.

Instructional Modifications

Some students would benefit greatly by doing assignments on a computer. The use of a laptop computer or a computer workstation could be helpful. Many students with disabilities and behavior problems have considerable difficulties with handwriting. Using a computer reduces that problem, although keyboarding may be slow. It also is a motivational method since assignments tend to get done faster, and the student has the advantage of being able to edit and correct before turning in an assignment.

A multisensory approach to assignments can be quite useful. Fulfilling some assignments in an oral manner helps motivate students with behavior problems to do tasks such as homework. Creating a mural, a diorama, or a performance piece that explains or includes elements of the concept to be learned is likely to result in greater learning and greater retention as well.

Physical Structuring

Seating assignments are extremely important. It usually is best to seat a child with disabilities and behavior problems in the least distracting seat in the room and that usually means up front. When I was a student, even if I began the school year seated in the back of the classroom, it wouldn't be long before I ended up in the front row. It should be noted, however, that some students with behavior problems do better seated in the back. If, for instance, a student tends to squirm and move around in his seat distracting everyone behind him, then a seating assignment in the back of the room might be better for him. Some teachers assign two seats and allow traveling between the two for students who have movement needs. If possible, seat the student next to another student who will be a positive influence. Also, it's not a bad idea to change the seat every now and then to provide some variety for the student. How often a change will need to be made depends on the individual student. Provide an alternate, more isolated spot in the room for a student to request or for the staff to request when concentration is particularly difficult. This option should not be presented as a punishment but rather as a tool to assist in completing tasks and projects.

Provide plenty of hands-on activities. This satisfies a need for movement and is motivating to the student. Alternate sedentary tasks with more lively activities. Try to get students with disabilities and behavior problems up and about from time to time as part of an activity. Activities should be scheduled for no longer than 20 to 30 minutes. For younger students (kindergarten through second-grade), 10 to 15 minutes may be the limit.

Instructional Levels

The most effective academic "modification" really is not a modification, but the way *all* students should be instructed. That is, all students should be instructed in a range of 95 to 97 percent *known* material and no more than 3 to 5 percent new or unknown material. This means building on existing skills. When students are instructed at their *independent* levels (more than 97 percent known material, which should be used for only independent practice), they become bored and may become disruptive. When they are instructed at their frustration levels (94 percent of less known material), they become frustrated, tune out, and may become disruptive.

Class Meetings

I have had a great deal of success having class meetings in my own classroom. We sometimes get so caught up in the academic part of school that we forget that socialization also is important. We need to devote class time to helping students with disabilities learn how to speak to others and negotiate for what they want. It has been my experience with class meetings that all the members of the class (including myself) learned a great deal about how to talk to each other and problem-solve together. Additionally, we learned how to accept people for who they are. This is particularly important for students who have disabilities and behavioral problems. Class meetings can provide an opportunity for students to learn about the disabilities of others. Students with disabilities can explain what it is like to live with a disability. These are skills that serve people well throughout a lifetime. I have observed many general education teachers benefiting from class meetings styled along the "town meeting" model. With larger student groups, the teacher must be more sensitive to assuring participation by all, but many teachers report that the students in their classes are more cohesive, tolerant of one another, and better behaved through the use of class meetings (Zimmerman 2007).

A class meeting serves many purposes:

1. It provides an opportunity for children to express their ideas, anxieties, and questions.

2. It gives students time to practice their verbal skills and their growing communications skills.

3. It enables students to interact with each other, to learn to listen, and to respect each other's ideas and comments.

4. It gives the teacher an opportunity to listen to students, to get to know them better, and to let them know their views are respected.

5. It is an informal setting, non-threatening to students, open for any topic they would like to discuss.

6. It is an opportunity to invite thoughts and discussions, raise questions, make suggestions, indicate possible directions of activities, introduce provocative ideas and make thought-provoking comments. Some suggestions will work, some will not. The leader can follow the children's response.

7. Meetings provide an atmosphere of community in which everyone can feel accepted.

How to have class meetings:

1. **Seat the class in a circle.** (A circle is best because anyone who is speaking is visible to everyone else.) Students can be seated on the floor or in chairs.

2. **Have students make up meeting rules.**
I would suggest no more than three rules,
i.e., only people with their hand raised will
be called upon, one person at a time talks,
students not talking will sit and listen without interrupting. By listening and rephras-
ing, the teacher can mold student
suggestions in these three rules. (Decide,
as a group, the consequences for people
who interrupt.)

3. **The meeting leader's job is to make
sure the rules are followed,** to encourage
dialogue, to help students learn to listen to
each other and to take turns talking, and to
give the students the opportunity to articulate their feelings and ideas. (The leader
should know everyone's name.) Unless the
purpose of the class meeting is for the
leader to get across an idea to the students,
the voices of the students will dominate the
discussions, not the leader's. The leader
may ask the class questions such as, "What
do you think of that?" or "Do you agree
with Clara?" or "Who would like to add to
what Jason has said?" or "Does anyone
know why that happens?" It also is the
leader's job to limit each student's state-
ment, so no one student is monopolizing
the class time. Some groups use a prop,
such as a phone receiver, which is passed
to the recognized speaker. (The leader can

be the teacher, social worker, or even a student under certain circumstances.)

4. **It is not unusual to have about 100 class meetings before you hit a good one.** Don't get discouraged! Keep in mind that even imperfect meetings can be very positive for the students.

5. **The first few class meetings should be short, no longer than 10 or 15 minutes.** Discuss the length of meetings with your students to see if they feel they are too long, too short, or just right. The younger the students, the shorter the maximum meeting length should be. Try to use the tolerance of the least attentive student as a guideline.

6. **Try to listen carefully to your students.** You will be a good role model for them in the process of teaching them to listen to each other. Using reflective listening not only will assure that you truly have understood the speaker, but will model an effective communication tool for your students.

Metacognition

We spend a considerable amount of time telling students with disabilities, who display inappropriate behavior, what to do and what not to do. We sometimes forget to tell them how to achieve what we ask of them, or we take for granted that they know how to achieve what we have asked of them. Sometimes there is a communication problem. Students may not understand what it is you are asking. Other times they may not see the need for changing their behavior and, still other times, the students are just not capable of performing what we tell them to do. We need to tell them how to deal with the feelings they are experiencing. Most individuals have a "little person" inside their heads that helps them to monitor their behavior. This "little person" may remind them to raise their hands before answering a question. For impulsive students, this "little person" may be tied and gagged and offers no assistance. The usual plan of action is impulse, then thought, then action. For many students with behavior problems they go from impulse to action. This leads to some serious judgment flaws and inappropriate behavior. By giving these individuals strategies and providing "a tool belt," or coping strategies, we assist them in making positive choices. It would be foolish to assume that during every situation an individual will pick a strategy from his or her "tool belt." However, if we don't give them a "tool belt" they will never have the option of choosing.

In terms of classroom action, the issue is how to teach students to discover and use strategies that will be successful in monitoring their actions. It is equally important to ensure that once these strategies are learned, they can be generalized across different situations. The idea is to teach the students strategies for planning and problem-solving in a way that will enable them to use their thinking processes to choose a plan of action that is successful or may be successful across a variety of situations and settings. What you really want the individual to do is to "social" problem-solve. However, you must provide the structure for that individual to be able to do that. Teaching children to talk to themselves (internally), to guide and mediate their behavior in a problem-solving manner, gives them that structure. Half the battle for the students with behavior difficulties is to come to some conscious recognition of their inappropriate behavior: what it is, why it occurs and when it occurs, or what stimulates it. Adults and peers can help by providing cues and prompts. It is important that the delivery of the message should be done in a firm, gentle, and caring manner. Students with behavior problems can be particularly sensitive to criticism. They can become over-reactive and even hostile when feedback is provided. This could be the result of an unquenchable need for reassurance and acceptance, or simply the fact that they have seldom received any feedback that was not negative in content. However, once students are aware of their inappropriate behavior, they can begin to formulate a plan of action.

Modeling procedures, behavioral rehearsal, role-playing, and other methods provide useful tools for teaching metaprocesses. From this perspective, the teacher's task is to provide the necessary instructional prompts by setting up situations in which the student can learn and practice newly acquired strategies. What is essential, for the student to be successful, is a plan of action that can be used to get through difficult situations. By teaching students metacognitive and self-monitoring skills we give them a fighting chance in times of stress. These are the essential skills they will need to be successful, not only in school, but in life as well. Below are some guidelines for teaching students metacognitive and self-monitoring skills.

Problem Recognition

It is important to teach children to understand and recognize different types of problems, and how their actions can cause problems. Very often a student with behavior problems aggravates or annoys another student without even knowing it. Later in the day, the aggravated student may "get even," leaving the student with behavior problems feeling confused and persecuted. It is useful to point out to the student with behavior problems all the factors that can cause problems. Sometimes a sensitive peer, particularly one who likes the student, can help accomplish this end.

Self-Monitoring

A good way to help students with behavior problems to be able to predict problems before they occur is to teach them to monitor their thoughts, feelings, and bodies and to recognize the "signals" that indicate a "plan" should be used. Often we feel things on a physical level before we feel them on an emotional level. (Some individuals breathe heavily and their faces may turn red when they are angry.) Students can learn what these physical signals mean and use them to predict their own behavior. (As a corollary to this, students can learn to "read" the non-verbal behaviors of others to better predict other people's behavior.)

Solution Generation

Teaching students to generate more than one possible solution to a problem will help them be flexible. I had a student with behavior problems in my class who had a horrific time in the cafeteria. We worked on a plan for him to talk to the lunch monitor when things were rough. I had spoken to the lunch monitor to advise her that this was our plan. The plan worked fine until this particular lunch monitor was absent. When a problem arose, the student, sticking to our plan, spoke to the substitute lunch monitor. Her response was to tell him to stop being a baby. He became enraged and furious at her, and at me as well. If he had had an alternate plan, when the original plan didn't work, much pain and disruption might have been avoided.

Anticipating Obstacles

As noted earlier, life never goes smoothly or how we expect it to all the time. That is why it is important to teach children to think of new "plans" if they encounter obstacles. One can seldom anticipate every possibility beforehand. Children with behavior problems should be encouraged to be creative when they encounter obstacles to their previous plans. Helping them consider the set of possible behaviors tolerated by others and the set beyond other people's tolerance limits will help guide them as they choose alternatives.

Consequential Thinking

Teaching children to anticipate the consequences of their actions is essential. It is vital that students with behavior problems learn that every action causes a reaction. They must learn to take responsibility for the actions they choose.

Visualization

Teach children to picture in their head, difficult situations for them, such as the cafeteria. Children should try and imagine all possible events, and they should imagine strategies for these events. Spending five minutes with a student with behavior problems and having him mentally visit the place he is going to can assist in preventing problems. Mental imagery is similar to running a movie in one's mind, but in this case, it is a movie over which one has complete creative control. In a sense, it is a type of useful daydreaming. The key here is to decide in advance what the desired outcome should be.

Relaxation

There are many methods of teaching children specific relaxation procedures and techniques. These are very useful for students with behavior problems, who usually have no idea how to calm down or relax. Telling them to calm down or relax is not enough. You must give them the techniques. A colleague of mine told me about a kindergarten teacher who taught his entire class basic yoga. Everyone, including his students with behavior problems, gained focus and calmed down.

Dealing with Anger and/or Frustration

Teach children to seek alternatives to aggressive behavior when they are angry or frustrated. It would be a mistake to tell children not to be angry or frustrated, as this sometimes is impossible. However, they can request to talk to someone, take a walk, count to 10, take deep breaths, scrunch up their toes in their shoes, or any number of actions preferable to hitting or striking others. Using a classroom mediation strategy, in which the entire class is trained to mediate disputes, can be very successful.

Self-Instructional Training

What you really want the student to do is to problem-solve. However, you must provide the structure for that student to be able to do that. Teaching children to talk to themselves (internally) to guide and mediate their behavior in a problem-solving manner, gives them that structure. They can start by verbalizing these steps to themselves:

(1) STOP!!! What is the problem?

(2) What are some plans?

(3) What is the best plan?

(4) Do the plan.

(5) Did the plan work?

Reinforcement

Using these metacognitive and self-monitoring skills is hard work for the student with behavior problems. It is helpful to encourage and motivate these students to use "plans" by reinforcing their efforts in using constructive methods to deal with their frustrations and problems, rather than acting impulsively.

Increasing Self-Esteem

Students with disabilities, particularly those students who have behavior difficulties, seem especially vulnerable to having low self-esteem. As the student grows older and starts to feel different from other students, he will compare himself unfavorably and will develop feelings of inadequacy. This is compounded by other students, and even adults, ridiculing the student. The best way to combat this is to start building their confidence before these negative feelings take hold. "It is documented that children and adolescents who have faith in themselves will be less likely to buckle under from outside pressures. The surer a child is that he is lovable and worthy the less security he will need from his environment" (Briggs 2001, p. 171).

The following are some suggestions for strategies on how to do this.

Assign Responsibilities

There are always a million chores to be done in a classroom and all students should have a part in doing them. For the student with disabilities and behavior problems, chores are wonderful. They provide a variety of activities and help make the student feel capable. All of my students had weekly jobs, but I always made sure there were extra jobs for those students who wanted and needed them. I always had three or four staplers in my room, as stapling papers was a favorite activity for many of my students. Errands to the office, opening difficult windows, and carrying things from my car to the class-

283

room were just a few of the extra chores. My students also helped the custodians, lunch monitors, and office staff. These opportunities provided them with variety, physical movement, change of scenery, and the gratitude of many people.

Assign a Buddy — Younger or Less-Capable Student

As previously mentioned, giving students with disabilities and behavior problems responsibility is an effective way to help them feel good about themselves. The responsibility perhaps most effective in improving self-esteem is an assignment to assist a younger or less-capable student. So often it is the student with disabilities and behavior problems who is the target of extra help, providing a painful reminder that the student is different and needs help. Reversing this situation, and allowing students with disabilities and behavior problems to be the helpers, lets them know that you trust them with responsibility of this nature. Letting these students know that you feel they have something to give is a terrific confidence booster. I know that many teachers are wary of sending a student with disabilities and behavior problems, who sometimes seems to be "out of control," out of the room to help others. It has been my experience that with the right groundwork, these students seldom let us down as helpers.

Assign a Buddy — Older Peer

Often students with disabilities and behavior problems display behavior that makes them undesirable to their peers so consequently they have few or no friends.

This is problematic since a major portion of our social skills is learned through peer groups. Students with disabilities and behavior problems may know the rules of adult society, but if they have no friends, they usually have no clue as to the social rules among students their own age. This can be a great disadvantage. A student who wears jeans even a half-inch shorter than the rest of the students in class can be socially stigmatized. Students with disabilities and behavior problems miss out on even more crucial social rules. By assigning an older peer to "buddy up" with the student with disabilities and behavior problems, primarily for socializing, the student gets a positive role model, someone to talk with, and, best of all, a friend. Asking an older student to tutor a student with a behavior problem is not the same thing as just hanging out. Most students with disabilities and behavior problems need to learn how to just "hang out." Eating lunch together, playing a game or sport, or just talking could have immeasurable benefits for both students. The buddy student gets the reward of being a sensitive and helpful person and, in the best of all circumstances, feels that he or she has gained a friend as well. A word of caution: Don't assign an older buddy who is socially inept and oblivious to the social rules of the peer group. Equally important is not assigning a buddy who may encourage inappropriate behavior.

Display Positive Verbal and Body Messages

Frequently some students scapegoat another student because they sense that the teacher doesn't like the student. Teachers who are verbally sarcastic or who make fun of certain students are, in essence, giving the other students permission to do the same.

Behavior Modification

The most common form of behavior modification is positive reinforcement. There are many different ways to provide reinforcement, and I have seen a variety of charts that are wonderful and effective. Although behavior modification is not always the best intervention for some individuals, it can be highly effective for others. When using behavior modification systems it is extremely important to incorporate into the plan how to slowly remove the modifications when the individual is ready to exhibit appropriate behavior without the system. I have used behavior modification record sheets in my own class and have strongly recommended them to teachers and other educational staff when I felt it was an appropriate intervention. Following are two examples of behavior modification record sheets. The first one is designed for a younger student or a student who has limited control and needs a great deal of reinforcement. The second sheet is designed for an older student or a student who may need reinforcement only once or twice a day (Zimmerman 2007).

STUDENT_____ DATE_____

BEHAVIOR MODIFICATION SHEET

	Act.1	Act.2	Act.3	Act.4	Act.5	Act.6	Act.7	Act.8
1. Put things back where they belong.								
2. Keep hands to self.								
3. Follow directions of teacher and staff.								
4. Remain quiet during work periods								
5. Complete tasks.								

- Student should easily be able to do two of the five goals on the chart; the remaining three can be more challenging.

- Student gets a checkmark for each goal achieved during an activity.

- The chart should be read with the student after every activity. Student should respond with a yes or no to each goal when asked if he was able to reach that goal.

- This should be done as soon as possible after each activity. This also may help the student transition to the next activity more easily.

- A daily and weekly reward can be given.

- Reinforcing rewards for the student could be the following: spending "special time" with a staff person of student's choice, extra free time, computer time or tangible rewards such as markers, crayons and food. In order to receive the reward the student should earn 80 percent of all possible checkmarks.

- Provide opportunities for the student to earn extra checkmarks. For example, staying out of a fight at the next table might earn an extra point on either goal number two or goal number four.

CHECKMARKS

NAME_____ TEACHER_____

	MON.	TUES.	WED.	THUR.	FRI.
1. Respect your classmates and adults.					
2. Walk in the room and halls.					
3. Put appropriate effort into assignments.					
4. Be prepared for PE class.					
5. Complete homework for mainstreamed classes.					
6. Keep your hands to yourself.					
7. Respect other people's property.					

COMMENTS

- Student should easily be able to do three of the seven goals on the chart; the remaining four can be more challenging.

- Student gets a checkmark for each goal he/she achieves during an activity.

- The chart should be read to the student before lunch and before he or she leaves for the day. Student should respond with a yes or no to each goal when asked if he or she is able to reach that goal.

- If a student gets all seven checks he should receive a small reinforcement (pencil, sticker, Life Saver or points toward a preferred activity).

- Offer a weekly reward. Since it is possible to earn 70 checks, achieving 60 should qualify the student for the weekly reward, which could be chosen from the following: spending "special time" with a staff person of choice, extra free time, computer time or tangible rewards such as markers, crayons, or food.

- The student should be able to earn extra or bonus checks for exceptional behavior.

- The student also may keep a corresponding chart that can be compared with the teacher's at the same point in time.

Behavior Contracts

Behavior contracts deal with disruption by rewarding desired actions and discouraging undesired actions. The contract serves as a commitment from both the educational staff and student, and requires that all parties work together (Zimmerman 2007).

Some guidelines that are important to remember include the following:

1. Contracts should be written in a collaborative process with the student and the teacher, and/or other educational staff, and should be written in a positive manner. Be certain to state those positive qualities or skills the student has, and if possible, how those qualities can be used to enhance success.

2. Expectations should be clear, simple and specific.

3. Goals should be achievable and specific. Consequences should be reasonable and do-able. Just as negative consequences should not be unduly harsh, positive consequences should not be too grandiose. Help the child generate a list of possible reinforcers and negative consequences.

4. Try to get as many people as possible who are involved with the student to have input in the designing of the contract. Parents, at the very least, should be aware that contracting is being done.

5. Contracts should be tailor-made to each individual student.

6. After the contract has been written, a conference for signing the contract should be set up. This conference should be direct, but not harsh. At the conference, the student should be asked what support he/she would like in working to be successful.

7. The behavior contract should not be viewed as a punishment, but as an enhancement. Help the student see that contracting defines not only his/her appropriate behaviors, but the adult's as well.

8. All parties concerned should adhere to the terms of the contract. Particularly, at first, reviewing the contract in the morning, before anything can go wrong, may help.

9. Everyone should have a signed copy of the contract, including the student and the parent.

The following are two examples of behavior contracts.

292

RICHARD THOMAS

Behavior Contract

POSITIVE QUALITIES	**AREAS OF CONCERN**
- Positive relationship with Ms. Smith.	-Striking others.
- Other students like him.	- Inappropriate talking.
- Can be cooperative and charming.	- Inappropriate touching of others.
	- Inappropriate behavior in halls and bathroom.

GOALS FOR STAFF TO ASSIST RICHARD:

- Controlling his anger by providing alternatives to negative behavior.

- Providing incentives for appropriate behavior.

- Providing alternative space when necessary.

GOALS FOR RICHARD:

- Special time with staff of his choice.

- Extra privileges.

- Extra recess time.

- Special activities (i.e., cooking).

293

Richard is a boy who has many positive attributes. However, at times, he engages in behavior that is both disruptive and inappropriate. Richard can earn things that he finds enjoyable when he is appropriate. There will, however, be consequences for negative behavior. When Richard is engaging in negative behavior the following steps will be taken:

1. Richard will receive a warning about the inappropriate behavior.

2. If the behavior continues, Richard will be asked to sit at a designated seat. He will be required to sit in this seat for no less than 10 minutes.

3. If Richard is unable to maintain himself at the designated seat, he will be required to go to a designated spot out of the classroom for a period of no less than 30 minutes.

If Richard exhibits overt aggression toward anyone, he will be removed from the class immediately. He will be required to remain out for at least one hour.

SIGNATURES:_____

_____

WILLIAM JOHNSON

BUS CONTRACT

William has been doing quite well in school this year. However, there have been some problems on the bus. In order to help William act in a safe appropriate manner on the bus, the following terms of this contract should be agreed upon.

William will:

- Follow the bus driver's directions.

- Stay in his seat.

- Keep his hands to himself.

- Refrain from throwing objects on the bus.

If William is successful in abiding by these terms he will earn the following:

- Time to play games (Legos, cards, etc.)

(After 5 school days with no referrals)

- Special time with a designated staff person.

(After 10 school days with no referrals)

- A lunch out.

(After 20 school days with no referrals)

William will earn these things at a designated time. We all hope that William can be successful and safe on the bus. However, if he is unable to improve his disruptive and dangerous bus behavior, William will lose the privilege of riding on the bus.

SIGNATURES:

Student_____

Principal_____

Teacher_____

Parent_____

Bus Driver_____

Oppositional/Respite Plans

When a student is continually defiant and constantly oppositional, it's time for an oppositional plan. An oppositional plan is a step-by-step therapeutic plan of action that involves giving the student choices of behavior. There are consequences and choices for each step (Zimmerman 2007). This plan also is used when a student is not being purposely oppositional, but is having a difficult time being cooperative. The student may need respite from the demands and stress of what is going on in the classroom. It is particularly important that this plan not be viewed as a way of "getting rid" of a student who is disrupting a classroom. When the oppositional/respite plan is utilized accurately, a consistency is built into the program that not only benefits the individual student, but also benefits the entire class. When oppositional behavior is occurring, the teacher will have a plan to follow and not have to "re-invent the wheel." This can relieve much of the anxiety and tension a teacher feels about inappropriate behavior. The oppositional/respite plan should be utilized for all members of the classroom, not just the specific student with a disability. When the plan is working to its maximum, students learn to utilize the plan with minimal teacher support. Teaching students when and how to use the oppositional/respite plan on their own has valuable benefits.

Following is an example of an oppositional plan used for a student with behavior problems in a junior high school program:

Steps for Dealing with Oppositional Behavior

1. When David is exhibiting oppositional behavior (not following a reasonable direction), he should be given two prompts (20 seconds in between warnings).

2. If, after the second prompt, the behavior continues, David should be told, "You have a choice of following directions or going into the 'stress-free zone,' (designated spot), for at least five minutes." When the time is up, have David verbalize that he is ready to join the group and follow directions. If he is unable to do so, he should remain in the "stress-free zone."

3. If David refuses to make a choice, explain that you will now make the choice for him and bring him to the stress-free zone. If David refuses to go to the stress-free zone, or

goes, and is disruptive, he should be brought to "time-out" (a spot outside of the classroom), for at least 10 minutes.

4. If David is not ready to join the group, he should remain in Time-Out.

5. If David needs to go to the "stress-free zone" more than three times during a class period, the fourth time he should go to Time-Out.

6. David should have the option of requesting to go to the "stress-free zone" and should be encouraged to use this option when he feels himself starting to lose control.

Behavior That Requires Immediate Time-Out Without Warning

1. STRIKING OR HURTING SOMEONE.

2. THROWING FURNITURE.

3. ANY BEHAVIOR THAT IS SELF-INJURIOUS OR DANGEROUS TO OTHERS.

A request by the teacher or staff for David to go to the stress-free zone or time-out should be presented in a non-punitive manner. David should be told that everyone wants to see him happy and safe. Statements that are appropriate to say include, "We're sorry you're having such a difficult time." "It seems you need some time away from the group." "We want to help you get yourself back under control so you can join us a soon as possible."

Teach other students how to give appropriate feedback when a student with a disability is bothering or upsetting them. Inform the other students what the specific disability is and how it affects that student's behavior. Ask the student with the disability if he would like to be included in this process or not.

299

References

Alberta Partnership on Fetal Alcohol Syndrome (2000). Guideline for the diagnosis of fetal alcohol syndrome (FAS). www.amda.ab.ca/cpg/catalogue/documents/obgyn/tas/guideeline.htm

American Academy of Child and Adolescent Psychiatry (2002). *Reactive attachment disorder No. 85.*

American Academy of Pediatrics (2001). Clinical practice guideline: Treatment of the school-aged child with attention deficit/hyperactivity disorder. *Pediatrics, 105*(5), 1158-1170.

American Psychiatric Association (2000). *Diagnostic and statistical manual of mental disorders* (Fourth Ed., Text Revision). Washington, D.C.: American Psychiatric Association.

Anderson, V. A., Catroppa, C., Rosenfeld, J., Haritou, F., & Morse, S. A. (2000). Recovery of memory function following traumatic brain injury in pre-school children. *Brain Injury,* Aug; 14(8), 335-341.

Atkinson, L., Quarrington, B., & Cyr, J. J. (1985). School refusal: The heterogeneity of a concept. *American Journal of Orthopsychiatry,* 55, 83-101.

Attwood, T. (1998). *Asperger's syndrome: A guide for parents and professionals.* London: Jessica Kinglsey Publishers.

Aust, P. A. (1994). When the problem is not the problem: Understanding attention deficit disorder with and without hyperactivity. *Child Welfare* (Vol. LXXIII, No. 3) (May-June).

Barkley, R. A. (1990). *Attention deficit disorder: A handbook for diagnosis and treatment.* NY: The Guilford Press.

Barnett, M., & Trevitt, J. (1992). *Attachment behavior and the school child: An introduction to educational therapy.* London: Routledge.

Baron-Cohen, S. (2001). The core deficits of autism and disorders of relating and communication. Special Edition of *Journal of Development and Learning Disorders* 5, 1, 47-75.

Barrin, J., Hanchett, J., Jacob, W., & Scott, M. (1985). Counseling the head injured patient. In M. Ylvisaker (ed.), *Head injury rehabilitation: Children and adolescents.* San Diego, CA: College-Hill Press.

Beck, A. T., & Emery, G. (1985). *Anxiety disorders and phobias.* NY: Basic Books Inc.

Bloomfield, H. L. (1998). *Healing anxiety naturally.* NY: HarperCollins Publishers.

Bogels, S. M., & Ziegerman, D. (2000). Dysfunctional cognitions in children with social phobia, separation anxiety disorder, and generalized anxiety disorder. *Journal of Abnormal Child Psychology,* Vol. 28, No. 2, 205-211.

References

Bowlby, J. (1952). Maternal care and mental health (Monograph Series, 2 World Health Organization, Geneva, 1952).

Boynton, M., & Boynton, C. (2005). *The educator's guide to preventing and solving discipline problems.* Alexandria, VA: Association for Supervision and Curriculum Development.

Briggs, D. C. (2001). *Your child's self-esteem.* New York, NY: Broadway Books.

Bruun, R., & Bruun, B. (1994). *A mind of its own. Tourette syndrome: A story and a guide.* NY: Oxford University Press.

Bruun, R., Shapiro, A., Solomon, G., Sweet, R., & Wayne, W. (1976). A follow-up of 78 patients with Gilles De la Tourette's Syndrome. *American Journal of Psychology,* 133:8 (August).

Burd, L. (2007). Educational needs of children with Tourette Syndrome. In T.L. Marsh (ed.), *Children with Tourette Syndrome: A parents' guide.* Bethesda, MD: Woodbine House, Inc.

Burgess, D. M., & Streissguth, A. P. (1992). Fetal alcohol syndrome and fetal alcohol effects: Principles for educators. *Phi Delta Kappan* (September 1992).

Campbell, M., & Cueva J. E. (1995b). Psychopharmacolgy in child and adolescent psychiatry: A review of the past seven years. Part II. *Journal of the American Academy of Child and Adolescent Psychiatry,* 34, 1262-1272.

Clarizio, H. P. (1991). Obsessive-compulsive disorder: The secretive syndrome. *Psychology in the Schools,* Vol. 28 (April).

Cohen, S. (1998). *Targeting autism,* Berkeley, CA: University of California Press.

Colligan, N. (1989). Recognizing Tourette Syndrome in the classroom. *School Nurse* (December).

Cumine, V., Leach, L., & Stevenson, G. (1998). *Asperger Syndrome: A practical guide for teachers.* London, England: David Fulton Publishers Ltd.

Deaton, A. V. (1994). Changing the behavior of students with acquired brain injuries. In R. Savage & G. Wolcott *(eds.), Educational Dimensions of Acquired Brain Injury.* Austin, TX, Pro-ed Publishers.

Deaton, A. V. (1995). Psychosocial effects of TBI: What to expect and what to do. *TBI Challenge* (Spring 1995).

Dewey, J. (1900). *The school and society.* Chicago: University of Chicago Press.

Dewey, J. (1902). *The child and the curriculum.* Chicago: University of Chicago Press.

Divak, J. A., Herrie, J., & Scott, M. B. (1985). Behavior management. In M. Ylvisaker (ed.), *Head injury rehabilitation: Children and adolescents.* Austin TX, Pro-ed Publishers.

References

Epanchin, B. C., & Paul, J. L. (1987). *Emotional problems of childhood and adolescence,* Columbus OH: Merrill Publishing Company.

Ewiing-Cobbs, L., Fletcher, J. M., & Levin, H. S. (1986). Neurobehavioral sequelae following head injury in children: Educational implications. *The Journal of Head Trauma Rehabilitation 1*(4), 57-65.

Feeny, T., & Ylvisaker, M. (1996). Choice and routine: Antecedent behavioral interventions for adolescents with severe traumatic brain injury. *Journal of Head Trauma Rehabilitation 10*(3), 67-86.

Feldman, C. (1994, October 7). Inclusion of disabled. *The Schenectady Gazette*, p. A 2.

Frances, A., & First, M. (1998). *Your mental health: A layman's guide to the psychiatrist's Bible.* New York, NY: Scribner.

Frick, P. J., & Lahey, B. B. (1991). Nature and characteristics of Attention Deficit Hyperactivity Disorder. *School Psychology Review*, 20, 163-173.

Frith, A. (1997). Asperger and his syndrome. In A. Firth (ed.), *Autism and Asperger Syndrome,* New York, NY: Cambridge University Press.

Ghaziuddin, M., & Butler, E. (1998). Clumsiness in autism and Asperger Syndrome: A further report. *Journal of Intellectual Disability Research,* Vol. 42, Part 1, 43-48 (February).

Gillberg, C. (1997). Clinical and neurobiological aspects of Asperger Syndrome in six family studies. In A. Firth (ed.), *Autism and Asperger Syndrome,* New York, NY: Cambridge University Press.

Gittleman-Klein, R. (1975). Pharmocotherapy and management of pathological separation anxiety. *International Journal of Mental Health,* (4), 182-198.

Gittleman-Klein, R., & Klein, D. F. (1980). Separation Anxiety in school refusal and its treatment with drugs. In L. Hersov (ed.), *In and out of school (pp. 321-341).* London: Wiley.

Goldstein, S. (1995). *Understanding and managing children's classroom behavior.* NY: John Wiley & Sons, Inc.

Greenberg, M. T., Kusche, C. A., & Speltz, M. (1991). Emotional regulation, self-control, and psychopathology: The role or relationships in early childhood. In D. Cicchetti & S. Toth (eds.), *The Rochester Symposium on developmental psychopathology,* Vol. 2. Internalizing and externalizing expressions of dysfunction (pp. 21-56). Hillsdale, NJ: Erlbaum.

Griesbach, L. S., & Polloway, E. A. (1990). *Fetal alcohol syndrome: Research review and implications.* (Report No. EC232650). Lynchburgh College, Lynchburgh, VA. (ERIC Document Reproduction Service No. ED 326 035).

Hallowell, E. M., & Ratey, J. J. (1994). *Driven to distraction.* New York, NY: Simon and Schuster.

Hansen, C. R. (2007). What is Tourette Syndrome? *In T.L. Marsh (ed.), Children with Tourette Syndrome: A parents' guide.* Bethesda, MD: Woodbine House, Inc.

Heckman, M., & Rike, C. (1994). Westwood early learning center. *Teaching Exceptional Children*, 30-35 (Winter).

Hewes, D. W. (2001). *W.N. Hailman: Defender of Froebel.* Grand Rapids MI: Froebel Foundation.

Hughes, D. (1997). *Facilitating developmental attachment.* Jason Aronson, Inc.

Kaiser, B., & Sklar Raminsky, J. (2003). *Challenging behavior in young children: Understanding, preventing, and responding effectively.* Boston, MA: Allyn and Bacon Publishers.

Kauffman, J. M. (2001). *Characteristics of emotional and behavioral disorders of children and youth.* Columbus OH: Merrill Publishing Company.

Kay Hall, S. E., & Geher, G. (2003). Behavioral and personality characteristics of children with reactive attachment disorder. *Journal of Psychology: Interdisciplinary and Applied*, 137, 145-162.

Kerbeshian, J. (2007). Medical treatments and healthcare professionals *In T.L. Marsh (ed.), Children with Tourette Syndrome: A parents' guide.* Bethesda, MD: Woodbine House, Inc.

King, N. J., Hamilton, D. I., & Murphy, G. C. (1983). The prevention of children's maladaptive fears. *Child and Family Therapy* (5), 43-57.

King, N. J., Ollendick, T. H., & Tonge, B. J. (1995). *School refusal; Assessment and treatment*. Boston: Allyn & Bacon.

Klin, A., & Volmar, F. R. (1995). *Asperger Syndrome: Some guidelines for assessment, diagnosis, and intervention*. Pittsburgh, PA: Learning Disabilities Association of America.

Koplewicz, H. S. (1989). Childhood phobias. In C. Lindemann (ed.), *Childhood phobias*. NJ: Jason Aronson Inc.

Kronenberger, W. G., & Meyers, R. G. (1996). *The child clinicians handbook*. Needham Heights, MA: Allyn and Bacon Publishers.

Kurcinka, M. S. (1998). *Raising your spirited child*. New York, NY: Harper Perennial Publishers.

Lehr, E. (1990). *Psychological management of traumatic brain injuries in children and adolescents*. Rockville, MD: Aspen Publishers.

Lentini, S. P. (2007). NCLB can and must be fixed. *New York Teacher* (April).

Lerner, J. W., & Lerner, S. R. (1991). Attention Deficit Disorder: Issues and questions. *Focus on Exceptional Children*, Vol. 24, No. 3 (November).

Lord, C., & Rutter, M. (1995). Autism and other pervasive developmental disorders. In M. Rutter, E. Taylor & L. Herso (eds.), *Child and adolescent psychiatry, modern approaches,* 3rd ed., (pp. 569-93). Blackwell Science, Oxford.

Marsh, T. L. (2007). Educational needs of children with Tourette Syndrome In: *Children with Tourette Syndrome: A parents' guide* (ed. T.L. Marsh). Bethesda, MD: Woodbine House, Inc.

McEwan, E., & Damer, M. (2000). *Managing unmanageable students: Practical solutions for administrators.* Thousand Oaks, CA: Prima Publishing.

McNamara, B. E. (1996). What every principal needs to know about ADD. *SAANYS Journal* (Summer).

Meade, J. (1991).Teaching a moving target. *Teacher Magazine* (October).

Mira, M., Foster, B., & Tyler, J. (1992). *Traumatic brain injury in children and adolescents.* Austin, TX: Pro-Ed Publishers.

Moss, E., St. Laurent, D., & Parent, S. (1999). Disorganized attachment and developmental risk at school age. In J. Solomon & C. George (eds.), *Attachment disorganization,* (pp. 160-186). NY: The Guilford Press.

Moyes, R. A. (2004). *Addressing the challenging behavior of children with high-functioning Autism/Asperger Syndrome in the classroom.* New York, NY: Jessica Kingsley Publishers.

Myles, B. S., & Southwick, J. (1999). *Asperger Syndrome and difficult moments: Practical solutions for tantrums, rage, and meltdowns.* Shawnee Mission, KS: Asperger Publishing Co.

National Head Injury Foundation Task Force (1988). *An educator's manual: What educators need to know about students with traumatic brain injuries.* Framingham, MA: National Head Injury Foundation.

National Institute of Mental Health (2007). Anxiety disorders. *www.nimh.nih.gov/health/topics/anxiety-disorders/index.shtml*

NYU Child Study Center (2007). About selective mutism – Profiles of silence. www.aboutourkids.org/about out.articles/about_mutism.html

Obsessive-Compulsive Disorder Foundation, ocfoundation.org (2007).

Parsavand, S. (1994, December 18). Inclusion changing education. *The Schenectady Gazette*, p. A1.

Peterson, A. L., & Azrin, N. H. (1992). An evaluation of behavioral treatments for Tourette Syndrome. *Behavior Research Therapy,* Vol. 30, No. 2, 167-174.

Piacentini, J. (2007). Behavior therapies for Tourette Syndrome. In T.L. Marsh *(ed.), Children with Tourette Syndrome: A parents' guide.* Bethesda, MD: Woodbine House, Inc.

Platt, R. (1986). Fear of attending school. *The Newsletter of the Phobia Society of America,* Vol. V, No. 1, 1-3.

Powell, A. (2004). *A school's guide to Asperger Syndrome*. London, England: Central Books Ltd.

Rabian, B., & Silverman, W. K. (1995). Anxiety disorders. In M. Hersen & R.T. Ammerman (eds.), *Advanced abnormal child psychology* (pp. 235-252). Hillsdale, NJ: Erlbaum.

Rapoport, J. (1989b). *The boy who couldn't stop washing: The experience and treatment of Obsessive-Compulsive Disorder*. New York, NY: Plume.

Reynolds, W. M. (1990). Introduction to the nature and study of internalizing disorders in children and adolescents. *School Psychology Review*, Vol. 19, No. 2, pp. 137-141.

Robertson, M. M. (2000). Tourette Syndrome, associated conditions and the complexities of treatment. *Brain*, Vol. 123, No. 3 (March).

Robertson, M. M., & Baron-Cohen, S. (1998). *Tourette Syndrome: The facts*. Oxford: Oxford University Press.

Rogers, M., Franey, M., & Smith, B. (2001). Using social stories and comic strip conversations to interpret social situations for an adolescent with Asperger Syndrome. In *Intervention in School and Clinic* (pp. 1053-4512), Vol. 36, No. 05, May.

Savage, R. C., & Wolcott, G. F. (1994). Overview of acquired brain injury. In R. Savage & G. Wolcott (eds.), *Educational dimensions of acquired brain injury*. Austin, TX: Pro-ed Publishers.

Schum, R. L. (2007). Selective mutism: An integrated approach. The ASHA Leader Online. www.asha.org/about /publication/leader-online/arc

Scott, J., & Cully, M. (1995). Helping the separation anxious school refuser. *Elementary School Guidance and Counseling, 29*(4), 289-298.

Shelton, M., & Cook, M. (1993). Fetal alcohol syndrome: Facts and prevention. *Preventing School Failure* (Spring).

Steingard, R., & Dillon-Stout, D. (1992). Tourette's Syndrome and Obsessive Compulsive Disorder. *Psychiatric Clinics of North America,* Vol. 15, No. 4 (December).

Stratton, K., Howe, C., & Battaglia, F. (1996). The affected individual: Clinical presentation, intervention, and treatment. In K. Stratton, C. Howe, & F. Battaglia (eds.), *Fetal Alcohol Syndrome: Diagnosis, epidemiology, prevention, and treatment.* Washington, D.C.: National Academy Press.

Strauss, C. C. (1990). Anxiety disorders of childhood and adolescence. *School Psychology Review,* Col. 19, No. 2, 1990, 142-157.

Streissguth, A. (1999). *Fetal Alcohol Syndrome: A guide for families and communities.* Baltimore, MD: Paul H. Brookes Publishing Co.

Swedo, S., Rapoport, J., Leonard, H., Lenane, M., & Cheslow, D. (1989). Obsessive-Compulsive Disorder in children and adolescents. *Archives of General Psychiatry, 46,* 335-341.

Talbot, M. (1991). Attachment. *The New York Times Magazine*, May 24, 1998.

Tantam, F. (1987). *A mind of one's own.* London: National Autistic Society.

Teitelbaum, B. R. (1979). Tourette - and teacher. *Kappa Delta Pi Record* (February).

Telzrow, C. (1987). Management of academic and educational problems in head injury. *Journal of Learning Disabilities*, Vol. 20, No. 9 (November).

The Child Anxiety Network (2001). Selective mutism. www.childanxiety.net/Selective_Mutism.htm

The National Center for Injury Prevention and Control (2006). Traumatic brain injury prevention tips. www.cdc.gov/ncipc/factsheets/tbiprevention.htm

The Tic.info. (2007). Tourette's at school. www.thetic.info/tourettes/school.php

Thurman, D. (2001). The epidemiology and economics of head trauma. In Miller L. Hayes *(ed.), Head trauma: Basic preclinical, and clinical directions.* NY: Wiley and Sons.

Tucker, B. F., & Colson, S. E. (1992). Traumatic brain injury: An overview of school re-entry. *Intervention in School and Clinic,* Vol. 27, No. 4, pp. 198-206 (March).

Turecki, S. (2000). *The difficult child.* New York, NY: Bantam Books.

U.S. Office of Education, Office of Special Education and Rehabilitative Services, Office of Special Education Programs (2003). *Identifying and treating Attention Deficit Hyperactivity Disorder: A resource for school and home.* Washington, D.C., 2002.

Waldron, T. (2000). Are psychotropic drugs overused in children? Therapists struggle with the implications. *Behavioral Healthcare Tomorrow,* pp. 14-19 (June).

Williams, B. F., Howard, V. F., & McLaughlin, T. F. (1994). Fetal alcohol syndrome: developmental characteristics and directions for further research. *Education and Treatment of Children,* Vol. 17, No. 1.

Wilson, J., & Shrimpton, B. (2003). Increasing the effectiveness of education for students with Tourette Syndrome. (Report No. EC 309 574 Melbourne University). (ERIC Document Reproduction Service No. ED 476 374).

Wilson, S. L. (2001). Attachment disorders: Review and current status. *Journal of Psychology: Interdisciplinary and Applied,* 135, 37-51.

Wolff, R., & Rapoport, J. (1989). Behavioral treatment of childhood obsessive-compulsive disorder. *Behavior Modification,* Vol. 12, pp. 252-266.

Wood, F. H. (1979). Defining disturbing, disordered and disturbed behavior. In F.H. Wood & K.C. Lakin (eds.), *Disturbing, disordered or disturbed? Perspectives on the definition of problem behavior in educational settings.* Minneapolis, MN: Advanced Institute for Training of

Teachers for Seriously Emotionally Disturbed Children and Youth.

Ylvisaker, M., Urbanczyk, & Feeney, T. (1992). *Social skills following traumatic brain injury.* New York, NY: Thieme Medical Publishers.

Zeanah, C. H., & Fox, N. A. (2004). Temperament and attachment disorders. *Journal of Clinical Child and Adolescent Psychology,* 33, 32-41.

Zimmerman, B. F. (1998). Classroom disruption: Educational theory as applied to perception and action in regular and special education. In A. Rotatori, J. Schwenn, & S. Burkhardt (eds.), *Advances in Special Education* (pp. 77-98). Greenwich, CT: JAI Press Inc.

Zimmerman, B. F. (2002). *The best fit: Creating the right LRE for your students with special needs.* Horsham, PA: LRP Publications.

Zimmerman, B. F. (2007). *On our best behavior: Positive classroom management strategies for the classroom (Second Ed.).* Horsham, PA: LRP Publications.